The
Balloon Shop
Memoir

The
Balloon Shop
Memoir

A Journey into the World of
Small Businesses

Abdulla Alkuwaiti
Fakhera Alkuwaiti

To | Aysha
Mariam
Ahmed
Mohammed
Saeed
Helal

v

Contents

Introduction

Toys, Toys, Toys; they're everywhere. They're in shopping malls, supermarkets and even gas stations.

Toys even came all the way to my house, right in the middle of our living room

Remote controlled cars, video games, small portable TVs and even small robots!

The magic of toys was everywhere. However, there were people standing between me and that magic.

Even though I was just a kid, I was a smart one. At least I was according to my mother!

It didn't add up in my mind. How come a shop makes just 2 dollars on a $20 video game? I was a kid and didn't know much about cost, revenue, profit and all that economic stuff, but I did know electricity and rent had to be paid.

Of course they Weren't obligated to give me a discount, but why lie about it? They insulted my intelligence. So I made a decision early on in life:

Business owners

However, life moved on and the older I got, the more attention I paid to my mom's advice:

I followed that advice and got high grades. On the surface, the advice worked perfectly; I got a good job that paid a good salary. However, beyond the surface, I didn't feel as happy as I expected to feel.

Section 1
I Quit

........................◆◆◆........................

I Quit

It felt nice. In fact, it felt amazing. I finally managed to show them!

Unfortunately, my happiness Was quickly cut short when I remembered her:

I placed my mobile on the dashboard and looked at it. May be if I stared hard enough, they would call me and offer to negotiate. I will play hardball in the beginning, but eventually, of course:

As you can imagine, though, that's not quite the way things happened.

Meet My Wife

"But, dear, do you know who got the promotion?" I said.

"I don't care," she replied. "You go back tomorrow, apologize and beg them to give you your job back!"

"Apologies ? Who ? Me ! to them ! Never."

Needless to say, our argument was very long and fierce.

My daughter walked into the room which gave me an idea: I would try and appeal to my wife's sensitive side. Let's see just how much she really loves me.

"But honey, you know how much I hated that job. It was eating me up inside. Don't you think my health is important? Do you want me to die young?" I asked her in a soft, pleading voice.

It worked! Her eyebrows untangled a bit.

I continued, "Besides we have enough savings to live well until I find another job. Don't worry I have an excellent CV, so I will find another job soon. What I need now is some time to relax. I need a vacation".

I finished up by throwing in, "I need you to support me", to seal the deal.

Section 2
The Idea

Vacation (Thailand)

That guy looked familiar. I knew him from school. He was the laziest guy in my class.

How on earth did he mange to sit in business class?
I made a mental note:

But, like all things we try to avoid:

The "wow, it's a small world!" talk started, which for me is really a comparison of who's going better in life. Not my favorite subject right now, considering I was jobless.

"So how are you doing? I saw you sitting in business class", I said nervously.

I tried to fix what I said by saying, "I mean, how did you manage to get a seat in business class? I tried but there were no empty seats."

He told me he now manages his father's shop and is visiting Thailand to buy some toys. A container he said.

"A container, you say? Hmm, that's good. Good for you!" I am sure my eyes Were bulging out like tennis balls. A container full of toys! That's a lot of toys for a small shop.

I thought my heart was filled with just about as much envy as it could take, but after he told me where he was staying, I realized I was wrong.

The root cause of my hate for him was his father. I'm sure you'll understand when I tell you what his father did for a living. You see, he was none other than the toy shop owner.

He was also very different from all the boys at school. I guess it was something that ran in their family.

The Taxi Driver

I collected my luggage and queued for a taxi.

I ignored his comment and pulled out my tablet.

"Ooh, Mister, you have nice computer, you very smart" the taxi driver said in broken English.
"Yes, smart but no money. That's why I am going to a two-star hotel, like you said", I replied with a yellow smile.
"Oooh, Mister, all smart people have big money", the driver said with confidence as if he was stating a fact.
"No, smart people 'should' have big money", I corrected him.
"But life is unfair", I added.
"Oooooh", the driver said.

The taxi driver seemed to be interested so I continued.

"OK, let me tell you something: I have a master's degree and have, or had a very good job, but my friend who never finished college flew with me here on the same plane. And you know what? He was in business class while I was squeezed in a small chair in the back of the plane." I said.

"Near the toilet, too!" I added after a brief pause.
"Ooohh!" the driver said again.

I expected some signs of sympathy on his face. There were none, so I continued.

"And to make things clear, he doesn't even have a big job in a big company. Do you know what he does? He sells toys in a shop!"

I started to laugh and repeated, "he sells kids toys and managed to fly business class! How funny is that?"

"So he business man", the taxi driver said.

I was surprised by the driver comment. What does that have to do with anything?

"May be you can say that. A small business man", I answered, laughing even more.

I was waiting for the taxi driver to start laughing with me but instead:

I stopped laughing. I glanced at his reflection in the rearview mirror; he looked dead serious.

"My brother owns two shoe shops in Bangkok. He is a millionaire. Every year he travel 2 times to Europe", the driver said.

Now, that was too much! I never felt financially comfortable enough to vacation in Europe, and I had a good job in a good company. How can somebody manage to do that, just by selling sandals?

"So why don't you open a shoe shop and become a millionaire like your brother?" I said sarcastically.

I glanced a grin forming on his face.

The Wisdom of Taxi Drivers

I kept thinking about my conversation with the taxi driver for the entire trip.

Everywhere I went I was looking at people's feet. How can you become a millionaire from selling shoes? I would understand if it was from a factory, but just from two shops?

Maybe the driver's brother is making millions in Thai currency, a million of which is just 30 thousand US dollars. Still, that's a very good sum of money.

Wandering in Bangkok

In Bangkok, there seemed to be a shopping mall on every block. Not to mention, hundreds of stalls between every couple of malls, selling everything from smart phones to socks. And yes, they were also selling shoes and sandals.

I started to think of one of the biggest mysteries I had faced since my childhood. Do these shop owners make money? They must, but how much? There were many things I didn't understand as a kid and as an adult:

The Idea

Now, educated and with 10 years working experience, I still couldn't figure out how money is made in a small business. I can run a department full of engineers but I didn't know how to run a small cafeteria.

It was time to unlock the mystery from my childhood. I made a decision:

I will open my own shop and see how money is made outside a paying job

This was the perfect time. I had no work commitment and I had some savings that could help me get started.

But there was an obstacle. My Ego.

There was a solution however; someone else could simply appear to be running things, while I was actually in control of everything behind the scenes.

I knew someone.

Telling my wife

I think I actually saw a vein popping in her forehead.

"Huh? I've heard this talk before. In fact, I've heard it TWICE, before", she said sarcastically.

OK, OK...I did have a small shop, before. Alright; two times before! But come on! Don't be so quick to side with my wife on this. This time it will be different. First, I have to tell you about my failed business ventures and then, I'll tell you why this time, things will be different.

Failed Business No. 1.

I didn't get into this one for the money. I was a fresh graduate and like many young people, I was an idealist.

During my college years, I felt the pain of paying hundreds of dollars for books, so had made a decision:

I will open a book store and sell books at a discount. knowledge should be free.

However, I didn't want to invest a lot, considering I didn't have that much to spend, anyway. That's why I found a small shop in the basement of an old building and filled it with "good" books. Books that are actually filled with knowledge, not the type of books sold in "commercial" bookstores, the ones that are mainly used to decorate coffee tables.

Unfortunately, my bookshop wasn't doing much selling!

Anyway, you can imagine how it ended. I could no longer support the business from my salary and after one year, I pulled the plug.

The thing that really upset me though, was that despite my good intentions and cheap prices, I was still seeing people buying from those other "commercial" bookshops.

Failed Business No. 2

A few years had passed. Since then, I managed to build my career and save up some money. I decided to start a business that suited my intelligence, so I then decided to:

> I will open my own training company!

The company that I worked for was spending hundreds of thousands on training. I decided to earn some of money in the training market for myself.

This time, I knew what I needed: A Management System. We always talk about how important it is at work. I hired a clerk and one instructor, who admittedly was low on experience, but had accepted a reasonable salary. I thought that he would learn with time, as most of us do.

I was very busy at the beginning because I was creating the management system. I tried to make it as detailed as possible; I even went as far as designing a form for the leave request. As for other matters like preparing the center and buying furniture, I gave my two workers the authority to decide. Besides being busy, I learned from work that successful managers must trust and delegate work to their staff.

Unfortunately, despite the management system, the company couldn't secure any training contracts.

I decided to use the instructor to do some marketing.

Yet, still no one came for training.

"But how can you be sure that the instructor really did distribute the catalogue?" my wife said.

"Why don't you go with him?" she added.

My wife suggested that I take few days off of work and join him.

Six months later, I closed the training center.

What did I learn?

So what did I learn and why would this time be any different?

From the bookshop, I learned that the main purpose of having a business is "TO MAKE MONEY". Without money the business will fail, regardless of how good your intentions were

However, it was business number two that taught me more. I learned that there is more to business than policies and manuals. There was something missing and I didn't know what it was.

What would be different this time is that I would start with the clear goal in mind of making money from a small and normal shop. No idealism or management theory now. The street vendors in Bangkok will be my role models. This time it will be the exploration and learning of the basics of running a small shop.

Back to the Idea

Honey, I will start looking for another job, I want one more chance at business. PLEASE HELP ME!

"OK", she finally said.

"Excellent", I said. "There's just one more thing; this time you will manage the shop".

"Me? Why me?" she asked suspiciously.

I didn't see that coming. I didn't want to admit that my ego wouldn't allow me to open a simple small shop.

"Becaaaause...., Because you are better than me in managing money! Just look at how good you manage the house budget." I managed to say, fearing she would reject the whole thing

I guess she liked my answer, especially the part about "a woman's touch". I could see her relaxing.

My wife's Idea

She placed her index finger on her lips, looked briefly to the ceiling and said: "Well, you know, I was thinking of opening a baby shower basket shop for a while".

"Baby shower baskets? Ah, you mean the gifts for new Moms?"

"Yes", she answered. A nicely decorated basket can sell for more than $100. My friends and I buy them all the time.

"We can also decorate hospital rooms of new mothers. That can generate big chunks of money", she added.

I didn't think much of the idea but my wife seemed very excited. She said there is money to be made, so why not try?

Market Research

The number one thing I hated about work was waking up early. I thought I got rid of that, at least for a while, until I find another job. But next day's morning:

"Other shop! " So we have competition already! Maybe we need another idea", I replied in a lazy voice.

"It's not just one other shop, I know at least 5 similar shops in town. Come on let's go".

42

"You spent half an hour with the salesperson and you didn't buy anything", I told my wife in the car after we left.

"So what?" It's a salesperson's job to take care of customers. Now, let's go to the next shop". She replied quickly.

Other shops

The next shop was similar, but with a section dedicated to making balloons. It was also busy with customers.

"Ninety dollars for twenty balloons!" I was amazed by the price, but the customer didn't even flinch when she heard it.

We went from one shop to the other till evening. When we got home, we immediately started talking:

That night we stayed up very late, talking about the shops we visited, what we can copy and what we can improve on in our own shop to-be.

The next morning -
Market Research, Again !

We went to the new shop, asking and investigating products and prices. My wife was paying good attention to details and making smart comments.

I liked my wife's observations. She was making a lot, while I had much less to say. I was afraid in time that she would hijack the business. It was my idea, after all.

I felt the need to add some value to the process.

First Conflict

In the living room I stood up and started to talk to my wife about my management theory regarding our competition:

She said nothing. Then she confidently:

Her reply was so unexpected and so assertive, that I didn't know what to say.

"We will charge like the other shops do. The price of bread is the same all over the city", she added.

A Place to Rent

I started to look for a place to rent. Prices were very high. In downtown, a small shop can cost up to 40 thousand dollars.

My wife suggested looking in newspapers.

Hey, check this out, this one is only 20,000 a year.

"So what did they say?" my wife asked excitedly after I finished calling the number in the ad.

"It is only 20 thousand a year, but they want 50 thousand for 'key money'."

"Key money?" she asked. "What is that? We can make our own key", she added.

"The guy told me that it's the money that I need to pay him to vacate the shop. This amount is totally independent of the annual rent", I answered.

Repeating Old Mistakes

I continued searching for a week. I woke up early each morning and drove around town hoping to catch a glimpse of a "For Rent" sign. Until finally

Let's go it's only $15,000 and there's no key money.

My wife didn't like what I found, though. "It's too far" she said.

"But the price is good", I argued, desperate for her agreement.

"It's cheap because no one will drive that far. People will go to other shops downtown", she said.

I knew my wife was right; The place had to be cheap for a good reason.

"I am so tired of searching. May be we need to forget the idea", I said.

"Don't lose hope now. It was your idea, remember?" my wife said.

Trying to encourage me, she added: "Let's go and sit somewhere to discuss it".

Section 3
The Kiosk

An Unexpected Location

We went to a coffee shop in one of the malls and sat in silence.

"Hey look there", I pointed at a stand (kiosk) selling flip-flops.

My wife looked and asked: "What?"

Me: Didn't you see? That lady was buying from the kiosk."

My wife: "OK…so?"

Me: "I never bought anything from a mall kiosk, before."

My wife: "Neither have I, so what's your point?"

Me: "Why didn't that lady buy the same product from the bigger shops nearby? I am sure there are more options there."

My wife: "I don't know. Maybe she was passing by and saw something that she liked. "

Me: "Didn't you notice that the number of kiosks is increasing in every shopping mall in the city?"

My wife glanced at me with a blank face for a few seconds. Then a smile grew on her face. I knew she liked the idea.

Excitement

We were very excited. The location problem was solved.

During the excitement, we figured out that a kiosk actually has many advantages.

Calling the Mall

To overcome the limited space in the kiosk, we decided to go for the mall closest to our house. That way we can use our house for storage and transfer products as needed.

I called the mall's customer service and received a big shock.

That was a big disappointment, but it made me wonder even more:

Intrigued or not, I couldn't justify paying that much for an adventure. Not while I was unemployed.

Death of the Idea

Over the following weeks the baby shower idea died slowly. We had some discussions here and there but they all ended with, "If only rents were cheaper".

I shifted my attention to searching for other jobs. Until one morning over breakfast:

"Who was it?" my wife asked
"It was one of my friends at company XYZ", I said smiling.
"OK, what does he want?"
"He heard that I quit my job and wanted to check if I wanted to join him at his company. He scheduled me for an interview, tomorrow."

The next day I took my family out to dinner. I told my family that the interview went very well and that I was offered to start work in 4 weeks.

But that wasn't the most important announcement that I had.

Why

"Why did you decide to go ahead with the business? Aren't you afraid we will lose a lot of money?" my wife asked.

However, her voice and body language were different. Not like the many "Why" questions she usually asks me:

It seemed that her question wasn't to tell me I had made a rushed decision, but to make sure that I am comfortable with it and ready for what was coming.

I guess she liked the energy that was generated by the idea of running a business together. The time we spent searching and investigating the business was very exciting and actually brought us closer together.

"I know I might lose a lot of money, money that I could use to buy my dream car but I think that I need to give this a try. I failed two times before because I wanted to do something different. This time I will open a normal business with a mind open to learning." I told her.

There was also another reason why I wanted to proceed with the venture:

I actually meant it.

Resurrection of the Idea

The new job got things moving again. I felt more secure to spend the money even though there was a big chance of losing it.

I had a month before starting the new job and all my attention was focused on the new business.

My wife called the mall's leasing office and made an appointment for the next day.

"He told me we need to make a business plan." my wife said.
"Why?" I asked. "It's not like they're giving us a loan or anything".
"I don't know. He told me that it's a requirement." she replied.

We were very excited.

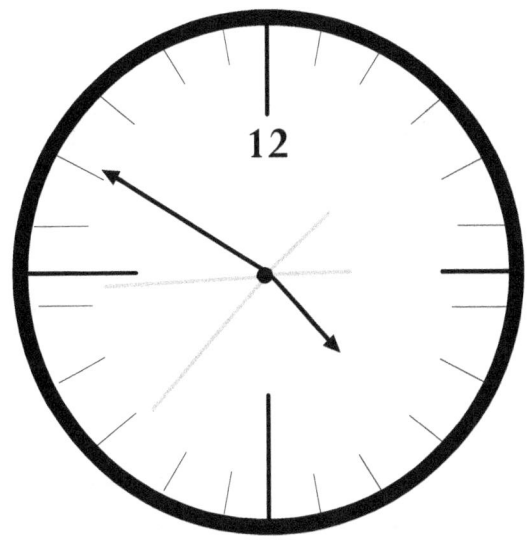

After few hours and a nearly empty paper:

Wife: "If we use flowers for decorations we need a cool space to store them. We can't do that in the kiosk."
Me: "I didn't think of that. Can we keep them at home?"

Trying to write our business plan made it clear that:

We jumped on the Internet and searched more on baby showers baskets. We hoped to find a kiosk similar to our idea.

"Why don't we use balloons?" I suggested.
"Why not? They certainly go better with kids than flowers do." my wife answered.

And just like that, we found our magic solution; using balloons instead of flowers.

Knowing more about balloons

We found that with balloons we can make arches, columns and virtually any shape.

"I think people will ask for balloon arches more, they will look nice in the hospital room entrances." my wife said.

"Yes and if some one buys a decoration, we could offer a few complementary balloons for free". I suggested.

We were up all night learning about balloons. We found much useful information:

- There are two types of balloons: latex (made from rubber) and foil (made from a thin aluminum film).

- We need to fill balloons with helium gas to make them float. A latex balloon will stay afloat - or seemingly fly - for 12 hours while foil balloons can stay afloat for about 3 days. Foil balloons can also be refilled and reused.

- We also found many videos demonstrating how to make balloon columns and arches.

- Additionally, I found a supplier for a popular brand of balloons and emailed them.

Ok we need to do 6 things:

1. Lease the Kiosk

2. Get a license

3. Buy helium gas

4. Buy balloons

5. Buy Teddy bears

6. Hire a salesman

So, as it went, we changed our business direction from flowers to balloons in a single night.

Leasing Officer

Today was our appointment with the leasing officer. I prepared a one-page business plan saying that we will be selling baby shower baskets and balloons. I also printed some pictures of balloon decorations.

I also prepared two checks, each for $12,500.

Visiting malls was a big part of my life but I never gave a thought to the people who ran them. That is, until I met Mr. G.

"We can choose our location? Wow, that's very exciting", I thought. Until, I started the actual selection process.

Mr. G told us to have a walk through the mall, select a couple of locations we want and then get back to him.

For every location there were advantages and disadvantages. "What if we choose the wrong location?" I asked my wife.

After a stressful three-hour hunt for a great location in the mall, we went back to Mr. G.

Mr. G's advice on the location

He told us the food court receives a lot of "foot traffic".
He pointed us towards two empty locations.

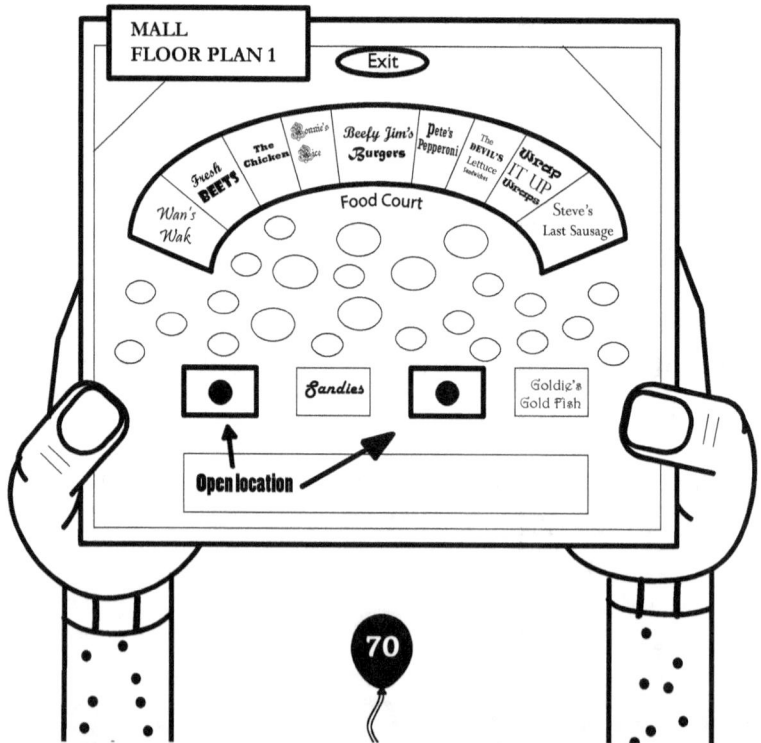

There are two locations, one in front of McDonald's and the other on the opposite side, closer to the cinema.

I suggested choosing the location closer to McDonald's, which is the one on the left, as I thought more kids would pass through there.

I was getting upset because my head was hurting. Really, I was processing too much information, with many possible scenarios. Also, my wife was correct; kids will be getting free toys in their happy meals.

Finally, we agreed on the location near McDonald's. After all, we were selling balloons not toys, so happy meal toys shouldn't affect our sale. In reality, however, there was no way to be sure. Any way we went back to Mr. G.

Once we were told that the location was taken, I wanted it more. All my doubts about it had disappeared.

My wife was particularly upset.

"I am sure he wanted that location for one of his friends", she told me.

As for me, I wanted to end the matter. There were many other things to do.

But there was one important thing I need to ask Mr. G before we finalized the leasing agreement.

Mr. G gave us initial approval to bring a helium cylinder into the mall. That was fine by me, but my wife insisted we get the approval in writing.

"But, dear, Mr. G will think we don't trust him. He gave us his word!" I told my wife and proceeded to sign the leasing agreement.

Finding Helium

The next day, I went searching for helium gas cylinders. I had no clue where they were sold. I used my wife's trick and called one of the shops that sell balloons. I tried to get him to tell me where they buy the cylinders from.

That didn't work.

I thought I could try asking in car repair shops because I see them use similar cylinders for welding.

After visiting 4 or 5 mechanics, I finally got help. One mechanic directed me to an industrial gas supplier.

He told me he can deliver the cylinders if I buy 5 at a time, otherwise I will have to do the transportation myself, which wasn't a problem for me because I have an SUV.

Getting Licensed

The Department of commerce had a big customer Service Centre, which was very crowded.

I knew my town was full of small shops, but it was the first time I had seen the people who owned them.

Seeing the number of people in the hall made me even more determined to open this small business.

We got a service ticket and waited for our turn.

I had mixed emotions while in the commerce department. I was embarrassed that after all these years I was going to sell balloons. I was envious of all those people who had started early and already had their own businesses. I also had a fear of failure, of course.

"Why do I need a permit from the sewage department?" I asked the officer.

The officer had a simple, non-negotiable reply: "Because those are the rules".

The officer kept listing the requirements. These requirements, and more importantly, the people who implemented them, made my life a real nightmare for the next week.

Name

Finding a name for the shop was easy. That is because I learned my lesson from one of my failed businesses.

For my failed training center business, I had spent $500 to design a logo for it, but saw with my own eyes how it did nothing to help me succeed.

So when my wife suggested the name "Balloon Art" I took it immediately.

"Aren't you going to hire someone to do the logo like you did before?" my wife asked.

"No, I will do it myself. I don't want to be distracted from the essence of the business. If we succeed, our success can be easily linked to any name." I said with determination.

"Wow, a new way of thinking!" my wife said with amazement.

I took the name my wife suggested, put 2 balloons on it and it was done.

78

Licensing

It was a very long and exhausting week.

We ended up paying $1,000 to get a license to operate. It was neither easy, nor cheap.

Buying Balloons

Today was my appointment with the balloon dealer I had contacted through the manufacturer website. He was an hour's drive away.

Based on the fame of the brand he was selling, I expected to find him in a nice shopping plaza.

The dealer's name is "Mr. L" and his office was an old desk inside a warehouse far away from the city center.

I felt comfortable with Mr. L, but my wife didn't. Nevertheless, he was our only option because he was the exclusive local dealer.

We couldn't argue with him

" So, how do the balloons feel?" he asked.

That was a strange question.

"Well, it was hard to blow at the beginning, but then it was easy", I said.

"They have a nice shape", my wife added.

He kept telling us about the characteristics of the rubber the balloons are made off and how they are the best in the industry. He even made us watch a video on how the balloons are made.

Listening to Mr. L

Mr. L spent the first hour telling us about how he started selling balloons and their different types.

He told us about the prices, which were very good:

Solid color rubber balloons were 15 cents each while the ones with designs cost 20 cents. As for the foil balloons they were from 1.5 to 3 dollars depending on size.

There was a catch though for rubber balloons. We needed to buy them in bulk or "wholesale".

"Wholesale?" I said surprised.

"Yes, if you will get into business, you should always buy wholesale", he said with confidence.

Seeing the surprise on my face, Mr. L explained what wholesale is:

"Wholesale means to buy many pieces of the same thing at a discounted price", he told me.

In our case, we need to buy balloons by the bag and each bag contains a hundred pieces. That does not seem to be a problem until you consider the wide range of colors available. There were a lot of colors, some of which I had never heard of before, like "magenta". Mr. L showed us the balloons catalogue and there were pages, after pages of selections.

rainbow of colors

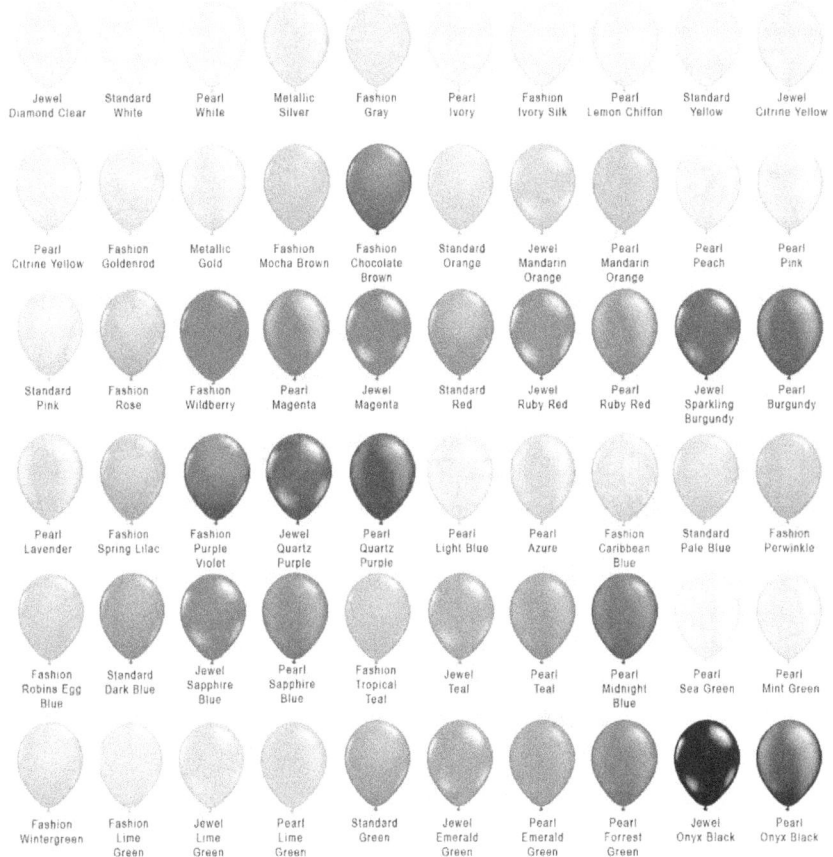

| Jewel Diamond Clear | Standard White | Pearl White | Metallic Silver | Fashion Gray | Pearl Ivory | Fashion Ivory Silk | Pearl Lemon Chiffon | Standard Yellow | Jewel Citrine Yellow |

| Pearl Citrine Yellow | Fashion Goldenrod | Metallic Gold | Fashion Mocha Brown | Fashion Chocolate Brown | Standard Orange | Jewel Mandarin Orange | Pearl Mandarin Orange | Pearl Peach | Pearl Pink |

| Standard Pink | Fashion Rose | Fashion Wildberry | Pearl Magenta | Jewel Magenta | Standard Red | Jewel Ruby Red | Pearl Ruby Red | Jewel Sparkling Burgundy | Pearl Burgundy |

| Pearl Lavender | Fashion Spring Lilac | Fashion Purple Violet | Jewel Quartz Purple | Pearl Quartz Purple | Pearl Light Blue | Pearl Azure | Fashion Caribbean Blue | Standard Pale Blue | Fashion Periwinkle |

| Fashion Robins Egg Blue | Standard Dark Blue | Jewel Sapphire Blue | Pearl Sapphire Blue | Fashion Tropical Teal | Jewel Teal | Pearl Teal | Pearl Midnight Blue | Pearl Sea Green | Pearl Mint Green |

| Fashion Wintergreen | Fashion Lime Green | Jewel Lime Green | Pearl Lime Green | Standard Green | Jewel Emerald Green | Pearl Emerald Green | Pearl Forrest Green | Jewel Onyx Black | Pearl Onyx Black |

My wife and I were speechless, but Mr. L, once again, came to the rescue:

He counted many colors. "How much they will be?", I wondered

He also told us to buy some foil balloons, hand pumps and a $200 valve for the helium cylinder.

"The total will be $2200", Mr. L said.

Advice from Mr. L

I think Mr. 'L' liked us or at east, he liked me, because my wife kept looking at him with suspicion. He was the type of guy who liked to talk a lot and I had no problem listening. In any case, he told us:

"The mistake that new business owners make is that they lower their prices more than the market. They will be happy because they will be selling, but when the time comes to buy new stock, they will not have enough money to do so and they will not grow."

He told us to sell latex balloons with helium for $3 and foil balloons for $5.

We brought the balloons home and started to explore them.

Starting to Understand, Maybe !

"I knew it", I said on the way back from Mr. L.

"Knew what?" my wife asked, surprised.

"Mr. L sold us each balloon for 15 cents and told us to sell it for 3 dollars. That means we will make a profit of more than 20 times the price of what we bought", I said.

"I knew that these business owners were greedy", I added with annoyance.

"With a buy-sale price difference like this we will make a lot of money", I told my wife.

Looking for an employee

"We will need 2 employees" my wife said.

I didn't answer her.

"Well, what do you think?" she asked.

"I agree. Especially if we have outside orders to fulfill", I replied.

"But even if there wasn't any outside work, we have to observe the working hours of the mall, which are from

10-10 every day of the week. We need two workers to work in shifts", my wife said.

My wife was correct yet, I was seeing the cost pile up. The cost of hiring a single foreign worker is about $3000, including the visa and fees. I convinced my wife to start with only one worker for the first 3 months and then hire another one. By that time things will hopefully be clearer.

I put an ad in the newspaper:

WANTED
Worker who can make balloon decorations for a new shop. Salary depends on skills and experience. Contact 1234567

We waited for few days, but no one replied to the ad.

Searching for a worker

"Why don't we try with party shops in town, maybe someone is interested in changing jobs?" my wife suggested.

"Is this ethical?" I replied doubtfully.

So once again, our detective work started.

We had only 3 weeks before the lease started and we were desperate for a worker. Eventually, we got few phone calls.

I suppose we weren't prepared to hire a professional, however. We were asking people to work full time for 3 months without a vacation and we didn't even know how much to offer as a salary.

Searching Continues

"Do you know why we cannot find a worker?" I asked my wife.

"Why?" she replied.

"Because we are looking for an artist and offering minimum wage, besides, no one is going to leave their job for a start-up business like ours".

"OK, so what do we do?"

"Let's change our approach", I said enthusiastically. "Let's look for someone without experience. Just a salesperson".

"Yes, and she/he will learn. There are tons of YouTube videos teaching how to make balloon decorations, she said agreeing.

We decided that since we're opening a kiosk, it would be better to find someone through another kiosk worker.

We went from one mall to another, talking with salespeople at different kiosks and distributing our number.

Talking to strange people and handing out my number made me very uncomfortable. It took some courage to do. My wife was the braver one. I didn't realize how brave she truly was until I saw here heading into a biker shop.

Our work finally paid out.

I was very happy. At last, someone is interested in working for us.

Meet Lia

The next lady, a lady came to the interview. Her name was Lia. We interviewed her at our kitchen table.

Lia used to work in a nursery, until her contract ended. She was looking for another job to transfer her work visa on.

She appeared to be polite. Always addressing me as "sir" and my wife as "Madam".

I didn't go through the questions in the interview sheet. I just wanted to finish.

Who is Keeping Records?

During our licensing process we accumulated many papers and receipts. There was also the rent agreement and bills from Mr. L, but the papers were scattered all over the house, in addition to the car.

To process the work visa for Lia, I had to go back to the government licensing office. That was something I wanted to avoid at all costs, but couldn't. Problems started right away.

The licensing office wanted our E-commerce card to process the visa application. I couldn't find the card. Without the card I had to pay 100$ for a replacement and had to wait for two days until it was processed.

I know it was our mistake to lose the card, but the licensing office had issued it. If they wanted to check it, they could simply do so on their system. Why did I have to bring it?

Going back and forth to the licensing office, made me bring a lot of negative energy into the house.

Fighting started.

Bringing a Helium Cylinder Home

We needed helium now, so Lia could start learning how to inflate balloons. Getting the cylinder inside my car was easy because the workers at the shop put it in for me. At home, however:

I put some rubber mats on the floor and slowly dragged the cylinder out of my car to the ground. The cylinder didn't seem to be damaged but the concrete floor cracked a bit.

But after half an hour of trials I couldn't screw the valve on. I called Mr. L:

Now, I needed to take the cylinder back to replace it.

I took the valve with me to the cylinder shop and managed to find one that fits.

But that night, I couldn't sleep.

Learning about balloon decorations

My wife sat with Lia everyday to teach her about balloon decorations. Actually, she was watching YouTube videos with her and to make sure she was practicing.

As for me, I was busy with other things. It seemed that my friends at the government licensing office wanted to see me more often.

It took me 3 days to finish Lia's work permit. When I came home on the third day:

I was very pleased. Lia seemed to get the hang of things very quickly. She made basic decorations, , but nonetheless, they were quite lovely.

Buying Teddy Bears

We needed to buy decoration items, such as wrapping paper and teddy bears. We immediately ran to the laptop.

We found many sites selling at a discount. We even found sites that shipped directly from China. For example, we found a teddy bear that sells in the mall for $30 priced at only $22. That price even included shipping! I was going to order but my wife suddenly yelled at me:

"The profit margin must be higher than that, think of

how cheap we got the balloons from Mr. L", my wife told me.

She was correct. The discount we got with Mr. L is almost 90%. Maybe there is another way to buy what we need. My wife suggested to give the decoration shops a try.

The discount was no good of course.

If anyone was going to help us now, it will be our new friend. I immediately rushed to the phone.

A wholesale market! He told me it is where small shops buy their stock from. I thanked Mr. L and planned to go there early, next morning.

The wholesale market

The wholesale market Mr. L told us about was an hour's drive away. We got there at about 10 a.m. and the place was buzzing with cars and cargo vans. The only parking space we could find was 15 minutes away on foot.

The market wasn't what I expected. For starters, there was no sign saying, "Welcome to the Wholesale market"! That kept me wondering If we were even in the right place.

It was very chaotic. Cardboard boxes were blocking walkways and although there were many people, no one was carrying a shopping bag. There were no kids either. It was very intimidating.

The shops were mostly on the smaller side and they were so packed with products, that I was afraid if I touched anything, I would be buried under a pile of those products falling on top of me.

Every shop had a desk or two with busy salespeople either talking on the phone, or writing bills.

We walked around looking for toyshops. We found a small one selling only soft toys. My wife and I took a deep breath and entered.

The price he gave us was the same as in the party shops.
Maybe we needed to ask differently:

That was still way more than what we expected. I felt the salesman was being untruthful because he took a little pause before telling us the price, while carefully examining us.

We found another shop and entered.

If the first salesperson was rude this one was totally unprofessional. She kept talking on the phone and ignored us, so we left.

While navigating our way back, we found another shop selling soft toys. I thought why not? Let's give it one more try.

72 $!! He must be kidding I thought. I acted as if I didn't hear him and asked again.

The sales man looked at me for a brief moment, I guess wondering if I was wearing a hearing aid; he then repeated what he just said but added one word:

My wife and I looked at each other. I swiftly pulled out my mobile phone and made a quick calculation: 72 divided by 12 is about 6$. Wow! I didn't even consult with my wife and immediately told the salesperson:

The salesperson made me pay the whole amount and gave me a bill.

He told us to come back in 2 hours.

Buying More

This first purchase boosted our confidence.

We discussed the situation and figured out that we needed to act differently in this market. We gave ourselves the following tips:

1- Look serious and don't act like tourists.

2- Use the word "dozen" when asking about prices. It's a "wholesale" market after all.

We also thought of the following trick: we will hold the bill of our first purchase clearly visible in our hand.

We thought that when salespeople see the bill, they will know we are "business people" and not just tourists.

We entered another shop selling decorating items and wrapping paper.

118

My wife found a very nice wrapping paper at a cheap price of $2 per wrapping paper compared to $5 in malls.

The salesperson told us we will get three colors: blue, yellow and silver in every dozen.

"So do you want to buy a dozen? You will get only 4 pieces in blue." I asked my wife.
"OK, the other colors are not bad either", she replied.
"OK, give me a dozen", I told the salesperson.

The salesperson studied us for a moment and asked, "So are you have a party?"

"No, we are opening a small shop for decorations", I said proudly.

"Shop owners buy by the carton, not the dozen" he said Condescendingly

He told us that if we buy a box the price will drop from $2 a piece to $1.65.

So we bought a box for $237!

Some Toys

We kept wandering through the market, found a couple of shops specializing in baby shower items and bought few baskets and decoration items. We - or rather I - also found some nice toys.

I insisted on buying two dozens of the spring toy.

Putting the stuff in the car

Our teddy bears were ready. The teddy bears, wrapping paper and baskets were all packed in either boxes or big blue plastic bags in front of each shop we bought them from.

At least the market had some carts for hire. One shop owner called a cart for us and told us it would cost $5.

"$15!!??" I didn't want to argue with the man in charge of the cart. I glanced at my wife and felt that she shared the same opinion.

So, I paid the man. One problem was solved, but now we had to put everything inside the car.

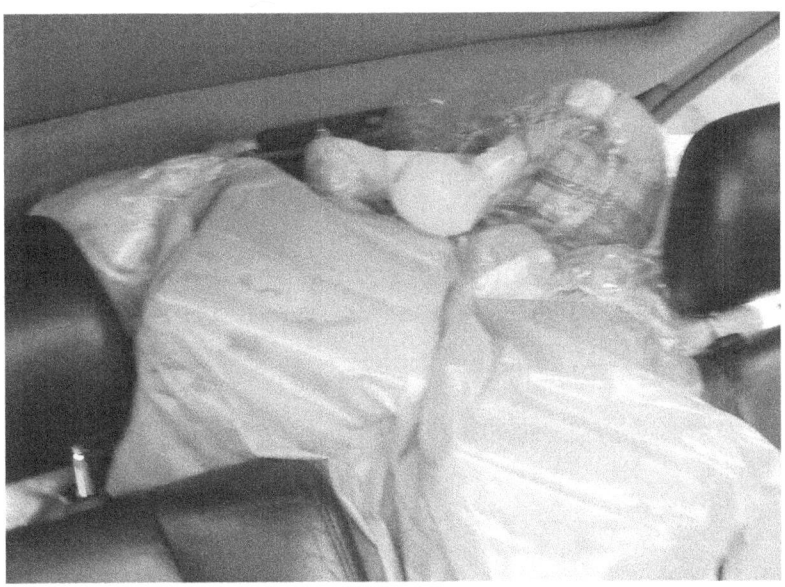

The car was so jammed that I couldn't see out of any window but we finally managed to make it home.

I wanted to leave everything in the car and go to bed, but my wife had other ideas.

Pricing

Buying items from the market was somewhat interesting. However, what followed wasn't. We had to sort, register and price the items we bought.

It was a tedious job requiring a calculator and a notebook. We had to go back and forth to the bills and try to decipher the handwriting of the salespeople.

I checked the bills and found that it cost 10 $ a dozen. Each one costs 83 cents.

Each toy we priced caused a conflict with my wife always increasing the price I suggested.

There were no rules to follow. How can we decide if a price is fair or not? Nevertheless, it was a new experience, tedious, but interesting.

Section 4

Starting

·············◆·◆·◆·············

Opening day

It felt great entering through the service door. It was 6 a.m. and it was so quiet and serene in the mall.

I felt special. Today, I wasn't entering the mall as a mere shopper, I now had a foothold in the mall; I am a businessman and that was official.

The kiosk was dark brown with 2 big drawers on each side. The wood seemed a bit cheap but I couldn't complain, not while a huge security supervisor was waiting beside the kiosk.

"I need you to sign a receipt for the keys. You can only bring stuff during the hours when the mall is closed." The supervisor said.

What's next?

I didn't mind the instructions from the supervisor. Actually, I wanted more, because I didn't know what to do, but he took the receipts and started to walk away.

"One second", I said. "Wait", I stopped the supervisor.

He paused, looked back and told me in a calm voice:

There was total silence while my wife and I looked at each other and the stand.

Thankfully, Lia came to the rescue. She started putting the little stuff we had on the stand. Two baby baskets, some teddy bears, a few toys and the balloons.

We started to help her and immediately realized that this was not easy. There were many decisions to make:

- Should we put the teddy bears with similar colors together or separate them?

- How do we prevent teddy bears from "sliding" off of the stand?

- Should we keep the teddy bears in their plastic bags? If we did they would not look as good, but if we didn't they could get dusty.

- On which side should we put the baby shower baskets, so that they are more visible?

- What about the toys? If we put them down, then kids might mess with them, but if we put them up, small kids would not be able to see them.

- Should we tie the balloons in one bundle or tie a few on each corner?

Silly questions? Well, they might seem so, but not for the person paying 25 thousand dollars to rent a wooden kiosk.

Not Enough Stuff

This was the only solution my mind could come up with.

"It looks empty", I told my wife after we Finished setting things up.
"Yes, we need more stuff."

There was a lot of empty space remaining in the stand. How come? The little stuff we had on it cost over $2000.

"I think we didn't arrange the items in a nice manner", I said. My wife agreed.
"So?" I said scanning the kiosk from every angle.
"So?" my wife replied.

Fear, Escape

We should have waited with Lia, but my wife had to take the kids to school. As for me, I had nothing to do and normally would be very happy to hang around in the mall, but not today.

To be honest, I was afraid of failing. I mean, I invested 35 thousand dollars in this project, while I'm unemployed. Did I take too big of a gamble?

The rest of the day, I tried to push the stand away out of my mind. I acted as if nothing special had happened this morning.

My wife was braver than I was, however. Women are more courageous than men. It's the truth, psychology studies support that idea. While more men try to avoid discussing their problem, women talk about them. Speaking of "talking", my wife was calling Lia every hour asking her:

"Do you have customers?" this will be a new sentence I hear my wife use a lot.

Day two

Since we lived very close to the mall, we agreed with Lia that she would come by the house every morning at 9 a.m. to make balloons in the garage, then I would drop her off at the mall.

Someone knocked on our door at 9:00, the next morning.

I stayed (or rather, hid) in the kitchen. After 5 minutes, my wife entered holding a small brown envelop.

$122, less than I used to make in 4 hours at my previous job. I was happy, though. In fact, I was ecstatic. We actually sold something!? Wow, this balloon business might actually work!

The Next Few Days

The next day, Lia brought $150 and the day after that, she brought $140. I was so happy and my immediate attention was focused on how to spend the money. My wife and I decided to take the kids out for dinner and do some shopping.

My wife, the kids and I had an amazing time

First Weekend

The first Saturday, Lia called my wife while we were having lunch.

She was moving fast toward the garage.

"There are many customers at the mall. Lia sold all the balloons and she wants another 25 of them", my wife told me.

It was very hot in the garage, over 100 degrees, but neither my wife nor I complained. Every balloon I made I thought of how much money I will be making

I took the balloons to my car and called Lia to come to the mall entrance to pick them up.

More Money

On Sunday, Lia brought $513. She had sold all the balloons we made, yesterday; 40 balloons in a single day

On Monday, Lia brought $430. Money was very good during the weekend. We were selling many balloons.

I made the following remark to my wife:

"During weekends people buy more."

It's simple, but I never thought about it before.

Wake Up Call- 1

Today is Tuesday, and I was waiting for Lia to bring the cash. I wasn't hiding in the kitchen any more. Today, I wanted to buy a new headphone with the sales' money.

"Why is it such a small amount?" I asked Lia.

"No customers, sir." she simply replied.

Wake Up Call - 2

On the same day Lia brought the $20, she told us that she needed more toys.

143

It hit me hard that the money I was spending these past days is not completely mine. The Business itself needed a part of it; a big part of it. Now, I need to take money from my bank account to buy new stock and helium gas.

Wake Up Call – 3

The next day we went to check on the stand. It was a shock

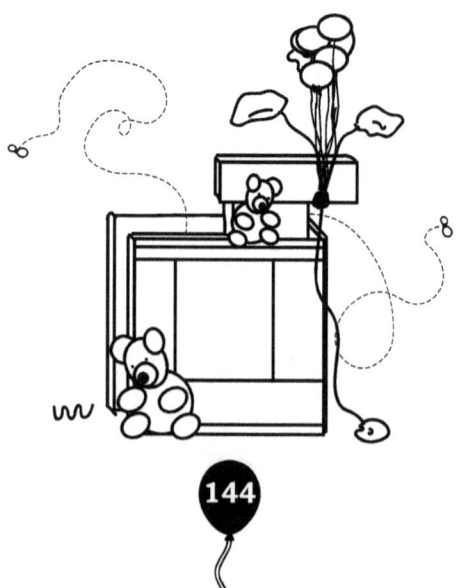

The kiosk was practically empty and many balloons were sagging and looking "sad".

My wife was very upset with Lia, that day.

"It's not exactly her fault that there's no stock", I told her.

The Reality of Business - Part of it at Least.

That week my mood went from sky-high to rock-bottom. When Lia was bringing the sales' money to the house, I was over the moon. My dream was finally coming true; I was sitting home and money was flowing in everyday.

Unfortunately, I realized that not all the money that came in was for me. I needed to put most of it back to in the business.

During my first week, I grasped some ideas about business. These ideas were not new to me as I had studied them while preparing for my Master's degree and had read about them online. However, they were abstract to me, until now.

Restocking

Today was a very busy day. I had to replace the empty helium cylinder.

My wife tried to warn me about the cylinder however.

The cylinder was indeed empty of gas but not empty of iron.

And I had to meet with Mr. L.

But it's OK

I had to wake up early and drive during the rush hour.

I had to carry the helium cylinder twice; once from the house and then back again.

I had to listen to Mr. L's stories, as well.

But, it was OK. There was one thing that made me accept all that.

yesterdays Sale

Cash was flowing in.

The Wholesale Market - 2nd trip

I was super excited for my next trip to the wholesale market. I liked shopping, especially for toys and I discovered during my first visit that the market is filled with toy shops.

When I was growing up I didn't have the money to enjoy toys as I wished; now I have the money but I'm a bit old for toys. My only way to work around that issue was my son:

Now, however, I can buy toys, and by the dozen !

My excitement to visit the market started the night before. I sat with my wife, so we could decide what to buy. She couldn't come with me, but told me to control my spending:

She gave me $500 from the money she was saving from our sales.

Shopping Spree

I wasn't taking a pen and a paper with me because that would take the fun out of it. The only paper I was taking with me, would be strictly for the purpose of showing off.

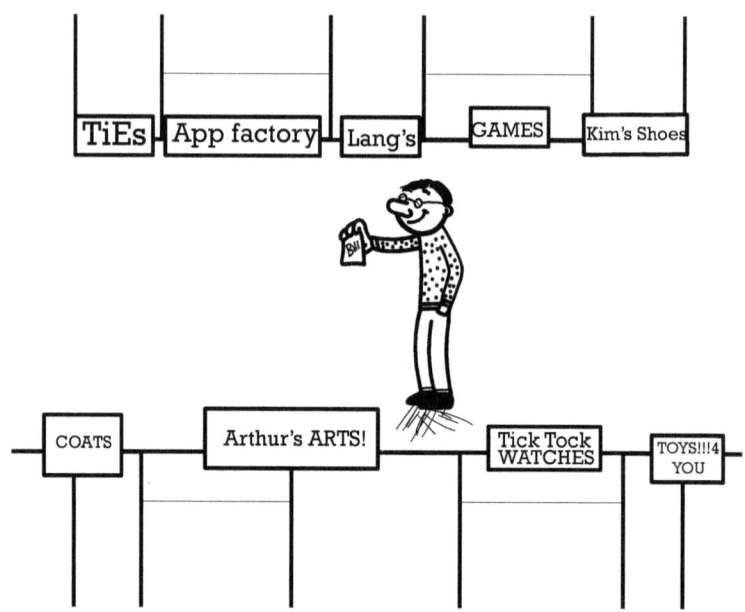

I took with me one bill from my last purchase.

I was discreetly, but intentionally showing off the bill at every shop I entered, just so they know that I am a legitimate businessman.

My first stop was the stuffed toy shop me and my wife first bought from, last time. The market was still new to me and it was intimidating. I needed anything to boost my confidence and nothing could do that better than a good first purchase.

The salesperson remembered me. I told him I wanted to buy more teddy bears.

"How many?" he asked.

I felt ashamed ordering only half a dozen. Half a dozen? Who orders just half a dozen?

I then went and bought 10 dozen spring toys. I also found some nice car toys.

I bought three dozen of those.

The Mugs

Wow, it was only 10 in the morning and I had bought everything I had agreed with my wife on buying (and a bit more than that!). I decided to keep exploring the market. I found these nice mugs with spoons attached to them.

They were on discount, $36 for a dozen, which was a mere $3 a piece. The original price was actually $72 for a dozen.

"A special offer? I have never seen something on sale in the market, before." I thought to myself.

What made me really want to buy them was their novelty.

I commended myself on my analysis. I was impressing myself more and more, each day. I am starting to think like a real businessman.

I told the salesperson that I wanted a dozen, but he refused.

"You can only buy a carton", he said.

There are 6 dozen in one carton. That was too much, I was going to walk away but the salesperson said:

"I have only one carton left, don't lose this opportunity"

I thought, "why not?" and decided to buy.

Unfortunately, I had spent the $500 my wife had given me.

Continue Shopping

I headed toward a nearby ATM and withdrew $2000.

I bought the mugs, but the shopping didn't stop at that.

Getting to know the market more

I made up my mind not to buy anything more. Actually, I had run out of money.

I found toy cars like the one I had bought at another shop.

I put on a triumphant smile and was about to leave, when the salesperson asked me, "But tell me, the ones you bought, are they full back?" he asked me with a grin on his face.

"Full back?" I didn't know what that meant, but didn't want to show it.
"Yes, it's a full..full back", I said in a shaky voice

The salesperson said:

"Full back cars are the ones that propel themselves when

you pull them backwards, I sell them for only $20 a dozen."

The salesperson smiled confidently and I left the shop.

Going home

This time I didn't think I would have trouble getting things into the car. After all, I could use the entire front seat, since my wife isn't with me. I was wrong.

I bought way more than the last time and I had no one to help me.

I stood for some time thinking while people were passing by and looking at all the toys near the car.

The parking lot was full and every 30 seconds a car would

pass by and ask me if I was leaving.

The only solution I could think of was to remove toys from their packaging and squeeze them in any way I can.

It was a stressful task and made me become very self-conscious about what I was doing and what people were saying about me. I am not used to this, where is my pride?

Finally, I managed to fit everything inside, I climbed into the car and was about to reverse out of the parking space, but wasn't able to. The way out was blocked by all the packaging I had thrown away. After 3 short trips to the waste bin, I could finally go home.

Return of the victorious

"How did you mange to buy all of this for only $500?" my wife asked.

"Actually, I had to withdraw a little more from my bank account, but it's our shop, our baby, our dream! Nothing wrong in investing a few more dollars in it", I replied.

"Here, look at these nice mugs I bought, they have a spoon attached to them."

"Wow, they're nice. Can I take some for the kids"

"Yes", I said proudly.

I handed my wife a bunch of crumbled bills and went to try one of the cars I bought.

The bills

The task of calculating how much each item cost and then putting a price sounds easy, but it isn't. Most of the bills were handwritten and it was difficult to identify which toy belongs to which bill.

My wife stayed up very late that night. It was my fault.

Arranging the New Items in the Stand

The next day I took the new items to the stand. Now, the stand looked really healthy.

The Laser

One afternoon, I grabbed my daughter's tablet looking for a game to kill some time. I found one and was enjoying my time until a red dot mysteriously appeared on the screen.

It didn't come from the tablet. It was my son.

I became very angry, snatched it from his hand and directly went to discuss the matter with my wife.

"Why did you buy a laser pointer for our son? Don't you know it's dangerous?" I said in an angry voice.
"I didn't buy it, he took it from the shop" she answered
"Which shop?"
"Our shop, the kiosk"
"What! Who bought it?"

She put her hands on her hips and said, "Make a guess".

It was me, of course, who else bought stuff for the kiosk? But I didn't remember buying it until I took a closer look. The laser pointer was attached to an action figure keychain. I didn't intend to buy the laser, just the keychain.

"It's your call. This is the last piece from the 4 dozen that you bought. Lia gave me this so that you could buy more, next time.

"Ten dollars? That's a big profit! I bought them for only a dollar and a half!" I said.

I cooled down a bit. "And we sold 4 dozen in less than a week?" I asked my wife.

"Yes", she answered.

I thought for a while and added, "But we shouldn't sell them. Kids will not use them for power point presentations". Money is a big temptation.

She kept quiet.

For the record, I can happily report that I didn't buy them

again. It wasn't easy, though. So much for labeling other people as being "greedy".

A Tip for Lia

For some reason Lia brought $720 on one day.

"Amazing!" I said in a voice full of joy.
"Give Lia the $20", I told my wife.

After I cleared my throat, I said "As an incentive, a bonus!"

"As a bonus for what? She's doing her normal work. Besides, it's too early for an incentive", she said firmly.

She told me about a worker in a beauty salon, whom she befriended lately:

Do you know they don't get a dime over their salary? She even gets paid less than Lia and has to dig her hands into women's hair every day.

My wife told me, that if we give her incentives now, we would be spoiling her.

"But dear, when I used to work, I used to get an annual bonus", I said trying to justify myself.

She didn't reply. Lia got nothing.

First month

Yes, it was official: 30 days had passed since we opened the shop. I knew we were selling, but how much? How much did we make in our first month?

My wife took the lead on this. Who else? If it was left up to me, I would never do it.

My wife brought the book that Lia had logged all the sales we made in. To Lia's credit, she had created that book without us even asking.

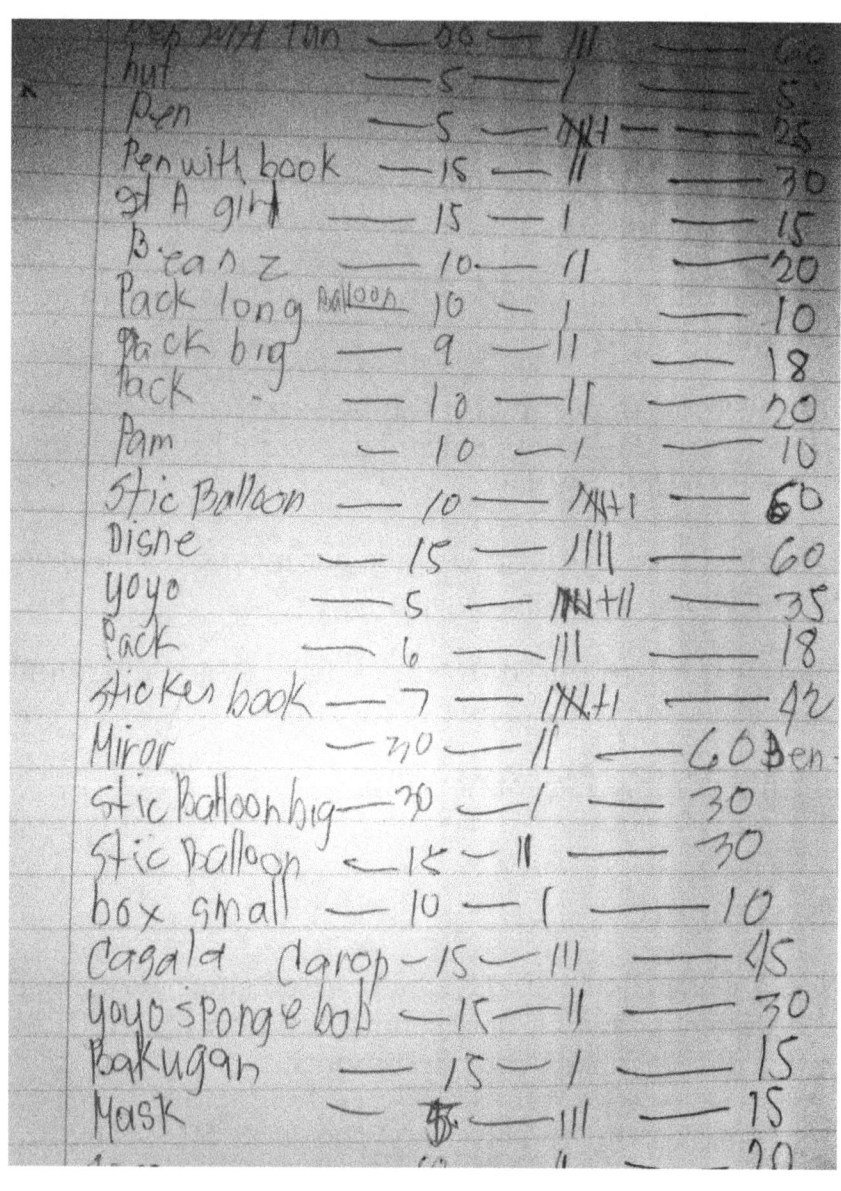

Item	Price	Tally	Total
... ... Two	00	III	60
hut	5	I	5
Pen	5	HHI	25
Pen with book	15	II	30
gt A girl	15	I	15
Bean z	10	II	20
Pack long Balloon	10	I	10
pack big	9	II	18
Pack	10	II	20
Pam	10	I	10
Stic Balloon	10	HHHI	60
Disne	15	IIII	60
yoyo	5	HHII	35
Pack	6	III	18
sticker book	7	HHHI	42
Miror	30	II	60 Ben
Stic Balloon big	30	I	30
Stic Balloon	15	II	30
box small	10	I	10
Cagala clarop	15	III	45
yoyo sponge bob	15	II	30
Bakugan	15	I	15
Mask	5	III	15
			20

My wife brought the calculator and started to work.

It was $11,239.

"Wow!!" I jumped in joy.
"Wait, we need to subtract the rent, Lia's Salary, the cost of the helium, the balloons.." my wife said.

My wife started to list all our costs.

Family and Business - 1

"Nothing", I said.

"Nothing? You're covered in sand from head to toe.

"I don't want to talk about it."

"Did you get into a fight?", she pressed.

"No, I wasn't fighting, but if you want to know it was windy today."

"So?"

"Make a wild guess. Balloons .....Wind ..."

I thought she would not stop laughing. When she finally managed to put two words together, she told me that my sister had called.

"She wants to order 75 balloons for the kids in her school", my wife said.

My sister works as a teacher in a nearby school. I was very happy. Finally, my family will start to recognize my achievement in business.

"Instead of $3.5, tell her we will do it for $3 a piece", I said.

My wife didn't respond to my discount suggestion. Maybe she doesn't want to give a discount. I felt the need to justify myself.

"Dear, it's my sister. We are family. They deserve a little discount", I said cautiously trying to secure her sympathy.

There was a moment of silence before she exploded

Now, I know that I said that they were family, but that was much too low. I know for a fact that no shop offered such a discount.

Family and Business - 2

I Mistakenly thought that my sister wanted to support my business, not just look for a good deal.

The school doesn't have a lot of money. Can you help me? Pleeeease?" my sister said to me.

I could see out of the corner of my eye that my wife wasn't very happy, but I reluctantly agreed to $2 a balloon. It was our biggest order yet and I hoped to get more orders from the school. To be honest though, my biggest motivation was my family. I wanted to show my sister that I cared to help her.

Honestly, deep down, I wantedto send a message to my family. That even though they didnt help me out with my business, I will always support them.

There was much planning to be done. If we inflated the balloons at my home garage, I would have to make 3 - 4 trips to deliver the required number of balloons.

I tried taking 30 balloons before in my car, and as you could imagine it wasn't easy:

I decided to take the helium cylinder in my car and make Lia fill the balloons at the school.

I raced to the garage to check on the pressure gauge. It showed a reading of 600

175

"What does that mean?" my wife asked.
"I don't know", I replied honestly

Blaming each other wasn't going to fix the situation. We had kids waiting for the balloons, tomorrow.

I managed to buy one cylinder before the shop closed. It cost me $320; 200 for buying the cylinder and 120 for the helium inside of it.

Delivery Day

We went to my sister's school at about 5, in the morning. I took the two helium cylinders with me to make sure that we don't run out of gas.

But we made it! The balloons looked very beautiful in that big bundle.

The balloons were handed out to the children who released them on the count of three.

That was it. So much effort went into making the balloons, just to see them disappear in the sky in under a minute.

My wife was correct. I could've only taken the new cylinder, but I wasn't thinking straight.

"So, where's the money? We need to buy some groceries.", my wife said.

"Oh, I forgot to ask my sister. She was so busy", I answered

Sister: Where is the Thank You? Where is the Money?

I felt great about delivering the balloons for my sister's school. I even dreamt about it.

When I woke up, I asked my wife, "Did my sister call?"

"No! Did she say she would call?" my wife replied.
"To thank me for yesterday", I answered.
"Your sister didn't call, but Lia did. Do you know why?"
"Why?"
"She told me she would be a couple of hours late because she felt tired from getting up so early, yesterday"
"Your sister's order caused a lot of trouble", she added.

About a week passed and my sister didn't call or bring the money.

"Did you call your sister?", my wife asked

"What? Oh, yes but her phone was out of service", Which wasn't true, of course.

I felt uneasy calling her to ask for the 200 dollars. She was my little sister, after all. I had my chance to remind her when I saw her at Mom's house.

"Oh, I am sorry! I forgot, but you know what? It happened so fast and the balloons flew off very quickly." she said

I did get my money a few days later, in old dollar bills and a few quarters. The cash wasn't accompanied by a 'thank you', however.

The Mugs

One day I come back from the mall and asked my wife:

"Do you know why we didn't sell any of the mugs I bought? You know, the ones with spoon attached to them."

"You really don't know" She asked
"No, neither did Lia. I asked her" I replied
"wait a second, I will make you a cup of tea in one of them"

She went to the kitchen and after 5 minutes she handed me one of the mugs.

"Here, enjoy" She said
She was standing close to me with her hands on here hips.

I tried to drink it but couldn't

"Its difficult to use it, the decoration is right were my mouth is supposed to be on the mug" I said to her.

I knew that I made a mistake buying these mugs. For left handed individuals they might be OK, but for most people its very difficult to use them

"But how could I possibly have known?" I told my wife
"You could have picked one in your hand before you bought them" She said and left the room.

The Pickle Jar

One day, my wife came home very upset.

"You mean 'our' shop. Why? What happened?" I asked.
"If it was mine, it would not look like a chicken farm!"

I opened it. There was a half-empty mango pickle jar.

"What is this?" I asked with amazement.
"This is what we are selling in our shop."
"We sell mango pickles?"
"Just look at the house and how clean it is", my wife said.
"Yes, but what does that have to do with the pickles?" I asked.

"If you don't believe me, just do the 'finger test'. Any place in the house, from the bathroom to the kitchen, I will pass."

"The 'finger test'? What is that?"

The Finger Swipe Test

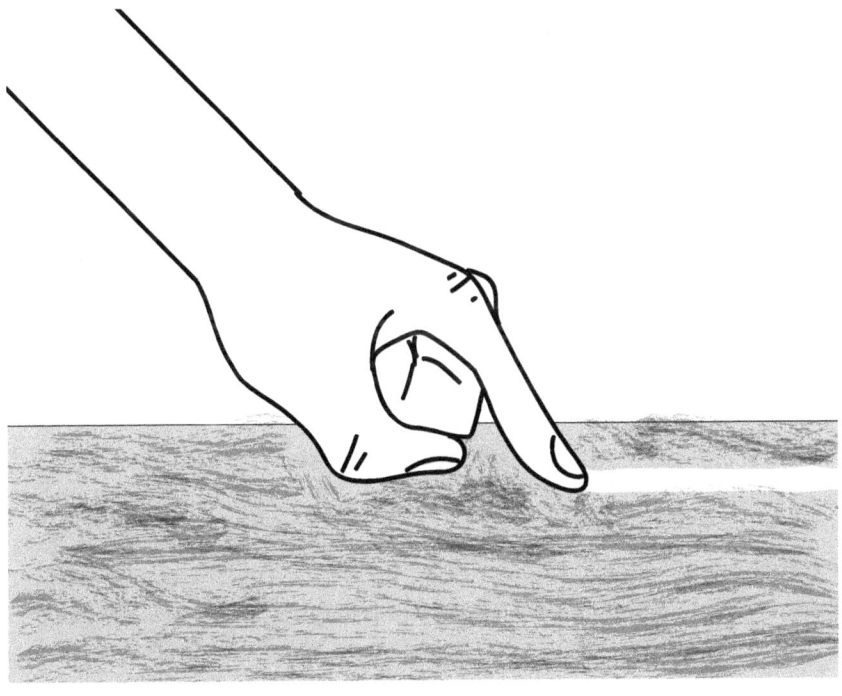

My wife did the "finger swipe test" on the surface of the stand and her finger was dusty.

"As for the pickle jar, it was behind the pink teddy bear!" my wife told me.
"Did you talk to Lia?" I asked my wife

"Just look at the other stands, they're so clean, you could eat off of them", she added.

My wife was right. Whenever I went to the mall early in the morning, I would see workers cleaning and dusting. A coffee shop in the mall had a huge cupboard filled with mugs for sale and I see workers clean them every day, one by one.

I really needed to talk to Lia about taking better care of the stand.

I sat with my wife and prepared a list of things to say like:

- This is unacceptable.
- You must clean every day, twice, at least.
- Every week, take all the items out, clean them and rearrange them.
- It's a small stand, it must look spotless.

In the afternoon, we went to visit the stand. There were no customers and Lia was talking with her friends who worked in nearby kiosks, another thing that greatly upset my wife.

I started going around the stand. In my mind, I was rehearsing the talk my wife and I agreed on. I faced Lia and I started to think about the pickle jar to get psyched up, but I don't know what happened to me.

I continued to think and Lia continued to wait for me to say something. Some serious thoughts came into my head.

What if she said she needs another person to help her? She has the right to ask for a day off. She doesn't even ask for a lunch break. She'll get better at work," I thought to myself.

My eyebrows relaxed and in a soft voice I said:

My wife was fuming. She didn't speak to me until we reached home.

"What did you do?" she asked angrily.
"What? I told her to clean up".
"And you gave her money? For what? To buy more pickles?"
"I was afraid she would get upset. What if she said she didn't want to work anymore?"
"Workers must be afraid of their managers, not the other way around".

I didn't know what to say. Was I afraid of Lia?

"With this attitude you will never succeed in business", my wife said, slamming the door behind her.

One More Happy Meal

One day in the mall, we went for a burger in the food court.

"Why the kids meal?" my wife asked.
"For Lia", I said
"Why?" she said with wide-open eyes.
"Because, because mm ..." I mumbled

I knew I made a mistake. Thank God I didn't order a regular meal for her!

"Well, because she stays in the stand for 12 hours. I want to be nice", I answered.
"You will spoil her like this. Look around you. Do you see other shop owners buying meals for their staff? She gets a salary and can manage".
"But, but....I already paid for the meal", that was the only response I could say.

I gave the meal to Lia, she smiled and thanked me. She also smiled at my wife, but it was a different type of smile.

The reality and the dream

Months passed with my new life as a shop (actually a kiosk) owner. Money was coming in and I was doing many trips to buy helium, balloons and toys. Still I was using my savings to support myself and my family.

As for the Job I was waiting for, unfortunately the project I was being recruited for was canceled.

I was enjoying the novelty of the wholesale market and the buying and selling experience. I was living in my own world and was consumed by toys and balloons.

I was busy on the computer searching about importing products from China. She left the newspaper on the table and left.

China

The small business experience was unfolding in an exciting way. Now was the time to go a bit further. Everyone was talking about visiting China for business, so that became my target.

At my previous work everyone was talking about china and how cheap things are. Every now and then, I would hear a story about someone making a small fortune by going there and bringing back some stuff to sell.

Dear, do you want to go to china?

Yes

She was very excited, but I told her we would not go to see the Great Wall, but to the wholesale market

"But are we ready?" she asked.

"Don't worry, I did my research and everyone on the net says it's the best place to go."

Any doubt I had about my visit disappeared when I spoke to the flight reservation agent.

Our destination was "Yiwu", which was 2 hours away by bus from the famous city, Shanghai. It was famous as a destination for small business owners. It has one of the world's largest wholesale markets.

In China

Our first shock came when we exited Shanghai airport.

That was about 150$. I thought China was cheap! I wasn't prepared to spend that much. I started to haggle over the price, but another customer came and took the taxi without haggling.

There were many taxis and they were moving fast. I was amazed at how people didn't complain about the price. Their clothes certainly didn't imply that they were rich.

At the end we paid the 1000 rimby's for the ride in an old taxi.

First Night

It was dark when we reached the city. Signs of life were limited to light traffic on the roads. I realized immediately that Yiwu is no Bangkok.

The hotel however, was nice and it was a bargain; only $60 a night for a 4-star hotel.

Futian Wholesale Market

The taxi driver seemed confused and asked me, "Number?" my wife suggested to use the Chinese name.

I tried to pronounce the name for him:

Still, we got no result. The taxi asked again, "number?"

I told my wife to try.

The taxi pulled to the side and looked at us. He pulled his hand and start counting the numbers on his fingers.

"One, two, three..", until six.

"Ah, he means there are 6 entrances" my wife said.

"What is the big deal, we can walk, how big can it be?" I said.

I didn't understand what the big deal was, the taxi driver could have dropped us at any entrance and we could have then walked. In any case I told him to drop us at number six.

The market was a huge concrete structure painted white, with white ceilings and white ceramic flooring. There were no decorations, seating areas or water fountains.

The most important thing was the shops. There were A LOT of shops, as far as your eye can see. The shops were small but filled with samples.

But we were surrounded by shops selling construction materials and hand tools. After walking for 15 minutes, we found ourselves surrounded by shops selling furniture. 15 minutes later, we were in the middle of shops selling cosmetics, then schools items, then suitcases ...etc. Everything you can or cannot imagine.

After an hour or so, we finally reached the toys section, which was at entrance number 1. That's why the taxi driver was insisted on asking which entrance number, the market is really gigantic. The first shops to great us in the toys section were the ones selling balloons.

There were balloons of all shapes and sizes. I was amazed by the variety of the designs. In the wholesale market back home, options were very limited.

"I told you we would benefit from coming to China. Just look at all the options we have", I said to my wife.

I pointed at one balloon and asked the selling lady, "How much?"

The sales lady took her calculator and typed 1.5. That was nothing. To reconfirm, I asked again, "1.5 Yuan?" she nodded.

"Wow. That's less than 20 cents, compared to 80 cents in the wholesale market back home." I said to my wife.

Why? Is she out of stock?

The saleslady talked to her friend sitting beside her, playing with his mobile. I figured out she wanted him to explain to us in English.

"Sorry Mr., This is whole sale market."

I felt offended. By now I thought I knew the "manners" in the wholesale market. You need to order in quantity. That's why I ordered by the dozen. When the saleslady saw that I didn't back down from my buying request she said:

3000 Balloons

3000 balloons? We quickly left the shop without saying a word. We found some chairs under a fake palm tree and tried to comprehend what just happened.

"That's like 250 dozen!" I said to my wife after making a calculation on my mobile phone.

"250 dozen! Wow, that's like … a lot!" she replied.

"But wait a second", I told her while using my phone calculator.

"You know what, at 20 cents apiece, that's only $250. A very good price", I told my wife.
"But how much will they weigh? How we will take them on the plane?" she wondered out loud..

She was right. Balloons are heavy, So that amount would likely weigh over 200 pounds, way more than our baggage allowance.

Yo-Yos

We didn't buy the balloons, however, we continued wandering through the huge market. We learned from the wholesale market near our town not to give up that easily.

Yo-Yos were hot at the time. There was a cartoon on TV about them and they were selling like crazy.

"Can I buy 4 dozen?" I asked the salesman, increasing the quantity hoping that he will agree.

Every carton contains 12 dozen, making a total of 144 pieces.

"If they are selling well, then why not?" my wife said.

"Try to negotiate with him. He might agree to only sell us one"

"No he will get upset. I don't want someone half my size to start shouting at me", I told her.

"Just give it a try! It's not like he'll bite. He looks friendly!", she said.

Well, he did look friendly, so I summoned my courage and asked him:

We didn't have two weeks to wait, though, of course.

The first day proved to be a big failure. We bought nothing.

Back at the Hotel

Our hotel was filled with foreign businessmen and women. The whole city was filled with them. So at dinner it was natural that we sat close to people who came to buy stuff like us.

206

Some Hope

The next day, my wife woke me up. She took the lead.

Minimum is 300 pieces.

Minimum is 10 cartons

You'll have to wait 2 weeks.

Sorry, Out of STOCK.

We were met with one rejection after the other.

Even my wife started to feel tired and lose hope. We decided to go back to the hotel. Our feet were hurting from all the walking we did. At the exit, we saw some nice soft toys.

207

A simple question like, "How much?" became difficult to say. The look we got from many of the salespeople when we said we wanted to buy a dozen was harsh. Their eyes were telling us that we didn't belong in the market but fortunately, this saleslady was different.

The lady was welling to selll us by the dozen.

Buying more

From that shop we bought 10 dozen mixed soft toys. We told the lady to give us a bill and that we would come back, later.

Our tiredness magically disappeared after our first purchase. We used the same technique we used in the wholesale market: Walking with confidence while holding the bill for everyone to see.

Suddenly it was easier to talk to salespeople and they were more willing to cooperate.

We also started to play some mind games inside the shops.

Of course, there was no container. I didn't even know how containers looked like, until I came to this city. But my wife and I were enjoying the attention this "bluff" was bringing us.

The toys we found in the market were very cheap, but what really caught our attention was the variety and novelty.

Our experience was changing for the better now, and I - of course - wanted to remind my wife of that.

Going Back to the Hotel

On the way to collect the soft toys we first purchase, we found a shipping office.

"Hey, let's check it out", my wife said.

We told Mr. Chen we wanted to ship 5 cartons.

That hurt, because it reminded us of how tiny we were in the business world. But we didn't want this to deduct from our happiness of today's achievements, so we just brushed it off and continued to pick-up our toys.

We went to collect our soft toys.

The thing with soft toys is that they are light, but can take up a large volume. Also, when you buy 10 dozen, they become heavy.

Of course, we had experience with dragging heavy bags, but not in a foreign country.

The only help we got from the saleslady was pointing the way to the exit.

There were no taxis waiting outside. We spent maybe 20 minutes looking at each other and at the people passing by. I hoped that someone would feel some sympathy and offer to guide us. We certainly looked hopeless.

Asking for help wasn't one of my strengths. Thankfully, a small truck approached us. The truck was so small, it looked comical.

I was tired and so I pretended not to hear her complaint. I gave the driver the hotel card and didn't even ask him about the price. He put our bags into boxs and he took off.

Changing Strategy

When we reached the hotel on the last day, we were too tired to realize what we did.

"How are we going to fit all of this in our luggage?" I wondered.

My wife said that we shouldn't buy stuff that we can find back home.

"Even if they're cheaper because we have a weight limit." she said.

She recommended we buy new and novel things like toys, that didn't yet reach our market. Doing that will enable us to sell them at a higher price and we will end up making a greater profit.

That was a good idea. Our goal was to maximize our profit.

That didn't completely solve our problem. We had already bought a lot of stuff. We cannot just throw them away. However, we pushed that to the back of our minds; we still had 2 more days for our flight back home. Therefore, the shopping continued.

Clap Watches

The next day we drifted a little from the toys section in the market toward the gifts and accessories. In one shop, we found watches that we didn't see before:

We liked the watches because they met our criteria:
- They were novel.
- They were light.
- They were cheap at only $2 apiece.

"We can sell them for $30", I said to my wife.

The sale man was willing to sell us only 300 pieces, even though the minimum quantity was 1000.

So we went ahead and bought the 300.

The market was full of new and promising products. We found some nice water bottles made out of thin plastic film:

STANDS LIKE A BOTTLE.

16OZ (480 ML) REUSABLE WATER BOTTLE

"Let's buy some. Schools are starting soon and these will sell well." my wife said. Unfortunately, the minimum order was 500 pieces according to the salesperson.

"That's a shame. They're cute and we can even give some of them to our kids", my wife said while walking out of the shop.

Seeing how my wife really wanted them, I felt the need to step in and show her how I'm a man who can make his wife's wishes come true.

"They are only made of plastic, how heavy could they be? We'll buy them", I said with confidence.

Going back home

We started to think of how to pack our luggage one whole day before our flight. We both knew it would not be easy.

We had 4 pieces of luggage between the two of us, with a total of 150 pounds allowance plus two carry-on bags with a total of 30 pounds allowance. But we of course, had much more weight than that and we didn't even need a scale to make sure.

"What are we going to do?" my wife wondered out loud.

I saw some commercials about this magic bag that you put your clothes in, and then suck out air using a vacuum cleaner.

"We can use that to carry the soft toys", I said.

We went searching for these bags in 5 different supermarkets, until we finally managed to find them.

Using these bags really helped a lot. The size of the soft toys we bought was reduced by almost one-thirds.

"But there's still so much left", my wife said.

"We will buy laptops bags and pack some stuff in them",
I told my wife.

I knew we would face a problem with our luggage
before I came to china. After all, I had experience in the
wholesale market. That's why I did my research and
discovered that passengers are allowed to take laptops
bags with them on the airplane.

"But we don't have laptops" My wife said

"So What, no one will check", I replied.

We bought the largest laptop bags we could find and
filled it with what we could.

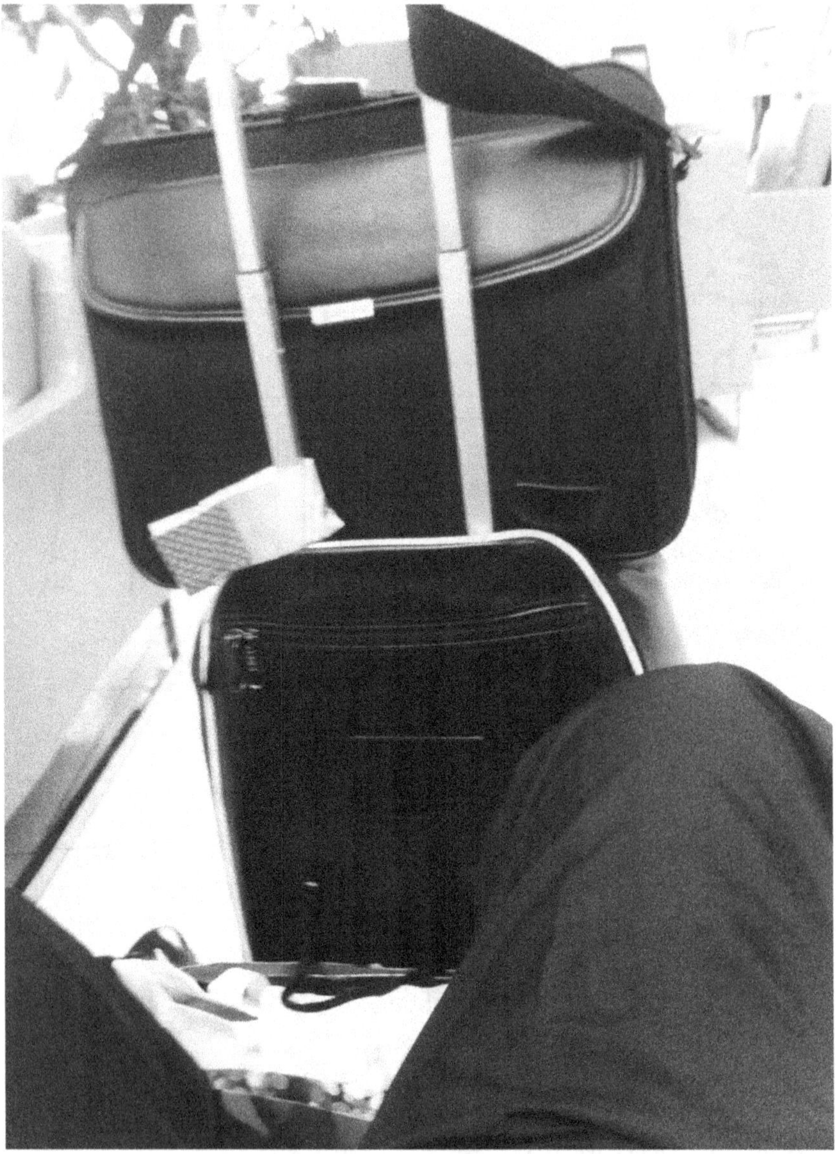

Packing the watches

"We still have so much stuff left. We didn't even pack the watches and water bottles, yet!" my wife said.

Of course, I had another idea for them. It was my last resort to ship them. The hotel called a representative of Chinese mail, who came directly to our room.

"Not allowed to ship battery in mail", he told us.

He was referring to the watches, as they were battery operated.

He gave us a solution, however. He removed the watches from the rubber bands and told us to ship only the bands.

We agreed as we had no other solution. We started removing the watches from their wrapping then removed the middle piece from the rubber bands. Alas, there were casualties!

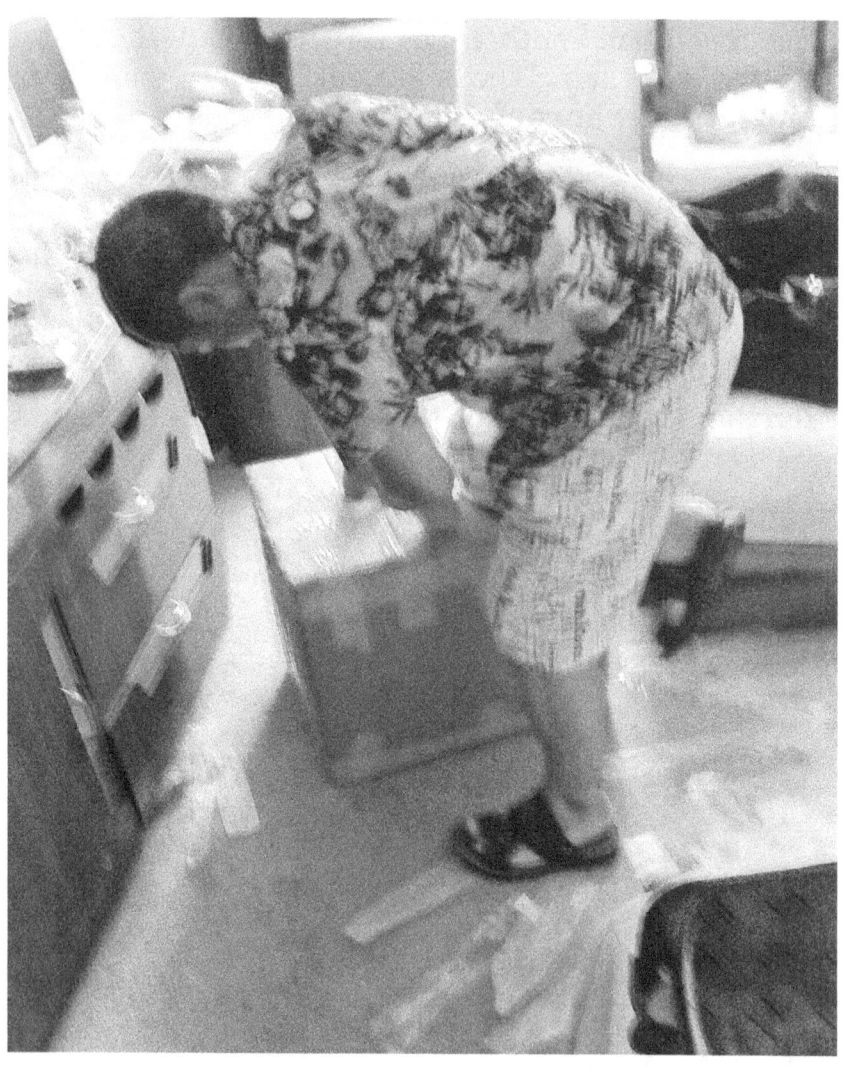

The bands filled half of the carton and we used the other half to put the water bottles in.

We couldn't fit all 500 pieces we bought. We only managed to fit 300.

But the mail representative took a measuring tape and started to measure the box

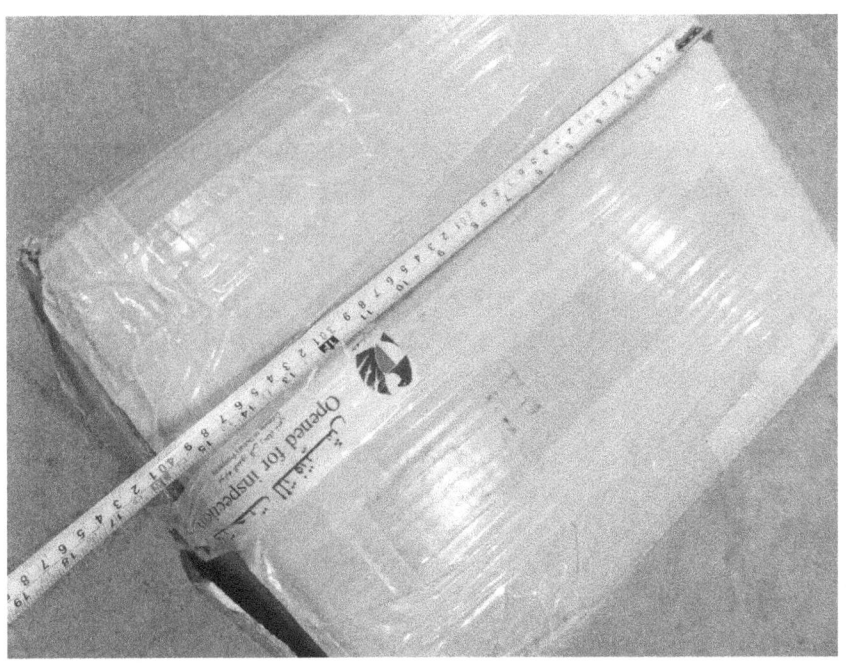

"What is he doing", my wife asked.
"I don't know", I replied.

"The weight is fine. It's only 20 pounds", I said.
"Sorry, too big", he said.

The box was bulging out about three inches in every direction and the mailing company rep couldn't accept that. He said that we could buy a bigger box.

The shipping cost for the box we had, which weighed 20 pounds was $120. If we want to, we can opt for a 32 lbs box for a cost of $260.

"The shipping cost will be more than what we paid for the water bottles", my wife said.

She was correct, of course. Each water bottle cost us a mere 10 cents.

We stood in silence for a while until the representative spoke in a loud voice:

" What you want to do ?"

We did what our logic dictated; we removed the excess water bottles, so we didn't have to pay for the extra shipping cost.

We ended up shipping only 100 pieces or so. We left the remaining 400 bottles on the hotel bed.

Still Have More Stuff to Pack

- We used vacuum bags.
- We bought the biggest laptop bags we could find.
- We shipped some of the items via local mail service.

Not to mention, our use of the largest luggage and carry-on bags we could find, but still, there was still stuff remaining to be packed. Not much though, as we were left with only the watches.

"What are we going to do with the watches?" my wife asked.

I stood silently thinking for a moment. Not because I didn't have an Idea, I had one - of course – but with this idea, I needed to be careful.

I took my wife shopping for a hand bag and got the biggest one we could find.

"But it will be very heavy", she Proclaimed.

At the Airport

The queue for the check-in counters was the largest I saw in my life.

As soon as we entered a man approached us:

We ignored him because he wasn't wearing a uniform and looked creepy.

At the luggage counter, the clerk told us our bags were 15 pounds over the weight limit. We had to pay $90 for each extra pound.

"That's more than a 1000 bucks! All the saving we could have made will be gone", my wife said.

"We didn't even count the cost of the tickets, the hotel, the transportation ...etc", she added in a very disappointed voice.

While thinking about my options of either paying for or removing the excess weight, the man who talked to us before approached me as if he was waiting for this to happen to us:

He didn't give me a chance to reply to him. He pulled our luggage from the weighing scale and started to pull things out of them.

"What is he doing? Stop him!" my wife yelled.

But for some reason I hesitated, and thought that maybe he could help us? I didn't want to pay $1000 for shipping and of course I didn't want to throw any more things of what we bought. I developed a strong attachment for them.

The man put the luggage back on the weighing scale and the weight was fine.

"But what about everything you pulled out?" I asked him, while pointing at the things he pulled out.

OK...now I understand his plan! He will put the extra stuff in the carry-on bags, which usually don't get weighted. But like I said, I had already thought of that.

It was like when you open a "jack in the box" toy.

Our carry-on bags were really REALLY stuffed. Things went flying all over the place.

The man was confused and didn't know what to do. He tried to put as much things in the carry-on bags as he could, but couldn't fit everything in. The remaining stuff he put in bags and handed them to us.

So now we had bags in addition to the carry-on and laptop bags. Not to mention, my wife's handbag, which was an entirely different story on its own.

My wife's handbag

Things moved very fast at the airport and no one bothered to ask us about the many items we were carrying with

us. That was until we approached the final check-point at the departure gate

"Stop! Stop!" an officer yelled at my wife.

They noticed that my wife's handbag was filled with watches. They told her to empty all the watches in a plastic box and send it again through the x-ray machine.

Thank God, I was watching from a distance. It was SO embarrassing. All passengers were looking at her.

"Why didn't you come to help me" She said, fuming with anger.
"I tried dear, but the officer told me to back away", I said lying.

Coming back

During the flight home, my wife just ignored me. She didn't speak to me even once. Her anger turned into excitement, though once we reached home.

The next day Lia brought 700, more than the average. Sales were good for the next 2 weeks, until we ran out of what we bought and I had to go back to restock from the local wholesale market.

Customer Care

It was Saturday morning and we were having a Family Lunch.

The mall's Customer relations officer called me and told me there was a complaint on the kiosk.

She told me Lia refused to sell balloons to one customer. Lia was just opening and told the customer not to bother her as she was busy.

"She gave me the number of the customer and told me to call him and apologize", I told my wife.

"Should we do that?" I asked her.

"Of course, we need to understand what happened", my wife replied.

She was very rude to me. No one has ever been rude like that to me before. I will take my business elsewhere.!

It was a difficult phone call, very difficult on my ego, especially. After all my education and experience, I am now apologizing to somebody I don't know about a couple of balloons.

243

Lia seemed very strong in her position and I kind of believed her. My wife, however, did not.

My wife didn't like my opinion. She had this believe that I always defend Lia.

More Lia

My wife and I became well-known to the shop-owners' community in the mall. We were the owners of the balloon stand, and that brought us great pride. One day while walking in the mall, however:

I thought the guy wanted to sell us some phone covers.

The phones' kiosk guy told us that the girl had cried.

He advised us, "Your shop is aimed at children. You need to be nicer to them".

Wow, that was very embarrassing. Our kiosk was making kids cry?

"But our shop must make kids happy. We sell balloons for God's sake!" my wife said.

The timing couldn't have been worse for Lia. It was the same week during which the incident had happened, when she refused selling balloons to that customer.

We went to talk to Lia, but she wasn't at the stand.

That just added fuel to fire.

"Break Time? Did you tell her she could take a break?" my wife asked me.

"No, but everybody needs a break, dear", I answered in the softest voice possible, But I don't think I sounded very convincing.

"Of course, everyone needs a break time, silly! But did she coordinate with us? I know she didn't coordinate with me! Did she do so with you? she asked.

Whose mistake was it for not specifying break times? It would be silly to think that during the last 3 months Lia wasn't taking break times. It just happened that we caught her at a bad time.

I hoped that Lia would not come until my wife get tired and left, but my wife was very angry. She was fuming.

So we stayed. While waiting for Lia a group of boys approached the kiosk.

"Look! That boy stole a toy and took off!" my wife cried.

I didn't know what to do.

"Don't just stand there! Go and catch him!" she said while pushing me.

But he was a kid! Am I even allowed to grab him? Do I make him pay for it, or should I call security?

I ran after him until I saw his father. He was twice my size and wasn't wearing glasses.

"Why didn't you catch him?" my wife asked angrily.

Lia with Mr. G

The incident with the boy stealing from our stand made me think before I go ahead and give Lia a warning, like my wife wanted. She had to deal with different people. Who said customers are always right? From my new perspective as a shop owner, I knew that customers could steal, be rude and mess with your stock.

I had to go and speak with her, though. In the mall, I met the leasing officer.

He was interested in talking about Lia.

"I heard many complaints about her. You might want to consider replacing her. The mall has its reputation, you know!"

That also didn't help Lia's case. I promised to talk with her and that no more incidents would happen.

"Let's give her one more chance, if she makes one more mistake, I'll fire her." I promised the leasing officer.

Straight away, I went to Lia.

"Lia, I know it's difficult to deal with customers, but I promised the mall management that if there are any more complaints about you, then I will have to find another worker", I informed Lia in a firm voice.

The party - 1

My heart fell into my stomach:

"It wasn't about Lia, thank God! It was the mall marketing department.

I was incredibly happy! Our shop became so famous, that we got calls to participate in events.

"I think it's the selection of toys we have. I have a good eye for toys", I told my wife proudly.

"Yes, and also how we display them. Last week I spent 2 hours rearranging all the toys with Lia", she declared.

The marketing lady said that there would be more than 200 kids in the party and that they would give us a table to sell whatever we want.

"Wow, 200 kids! We will make a lot of money!" my wife said, enthusiastically.

"But there is one thing...", I said, interrupting her excitement.

The marketing lady told me that in order to participate, I needed to donate 200 toys to the event.

"We have cheap toys like the small teddy bears we bought for 1.25 each. We can use those and we will make a bigger profit from the event. I am sure", I said enthusiastically.

"That's a good idea! I mean using the small teddy bears, but..."

"But, what?"

"But if we give out toys for free, the kids will not buy from us." she pointed out.

I didn't think of what my wife said, I had already made the decision. I didn't want to lose this opportunity. I need to act fast because the marketing lady had told me:

"I will call her now, 5 minutes have already passed!" I told my wife.

"Wait, we need to discuss this further", my wife said.

I called the marketing lady, anyway and delivered the 200 teddy bear that very same day.

The party - 2

200 small teddy bears at $1.25 came to 250 dollars. It wasn't cheap, but there was a big chance to make profit off of it. I knew from experience that the more kids we had in the mall, the more sales we would probably make. Some schools bring kids on road trips to the mall and on these days, we usually make around $500-700 easily, even if it's in the middle of the week.

I was extremely happy that I didn't let the opportunity pass.

"The event will be from 7 to 9 pm. Who will stay in the kiosk?" my wife asked.

I didn't think of that. We can't just close at that time, it's against the mall's policy.

It's their event, I think they will allow you to close for a couple of hours, my wife said.

"But I don't want them to know that I have only one worker", I replied.

We decided to check with Lia.

Don't worry sir, I will tell my friend to cover for me.

This is what I like about Lia; she never complains about additional work.

Lia told her friend who worked in the adjacent sweets' kiosk to cover for her

"Can she do it? Can we trust her friend?", my wife asked.

"Don't worry! I am sure they always cover for each other", I said

The party - 3

The party was held at a hotel. On the day of the event, I put the helium cylinder in my car in addition to 3 large boxes filled with toys.

I waited in the parking lot for almost an hour but Lia didn't call.

257

"I think she is busy selling, 200 Kids are a lot", I thought to myself.

The party - 4

"Hi, you're back soon. How did it go?" My wife said.

I handed my wife the money we made.

"The party lasted for only an hour and started off by giving out the free toys we supplied", I told my wife.
"You were right. If there are free toys, the kids won't buy any more with their money".

I am not mad about the 200 teddy bears we gave out, but the effort and time wasted in going and coming back from the party.

However, what really got to me was how stupid I was. I fell for the oldest trick in the marketing book. When the marketing lady told me "don't waste the opportunity" and " get back to me in 5 minutes", she was playing with my mind.

"I think the mall tricked us. They wanted to get free gifts for their event", my wife said.

Although I agreed with my wife's analysis, I didn't discount the whole experience as a failure.

"But you know what? At least we held our end of the deal with the mall and provided the free gifts. I am sure they will appreciate that and in any coming event where they need balloons, we will be on top of their list", I said.

The party - 5

The next day, when Lia came to my house to make balloons she handed me one envelope.

"This is yesterday's sale from my friend", she told me

The envelope was sealed.

"See how honest Lia is? She could have told us that her friend made no sales, since it was only for few hours", I told my wife in an attempt to soften her feelings towards Lia

However, when we opened the envelope we were both in shock.

This started a long discussion

"How come she sold more than double the usual in just 4 hours?" my wife asked.

During weekdays, Lia's sale averaged only $100.

"I don't know", I said.
"Is she stealing?" my wife asked.
"Maybe it's how she treats customers. She doesn't invite them to buy", my wife said, providing another reasoning.

That made much more sense to me. The idea that Lia was stealing from us was difficult for me to believe, as she was doing a good job logging sales every day. However, the idea it might be that she is not welcoming customers and not nice with kids.

"We need to replace her with a salesperson who has good sales skills", my wife said.

I kept quiet.

The party - 6 (The betrayal)

A few days after the party, I saw the following in the mall:

If I didn't see it with my own eyes, I would not have believed it. Two men were filling balloons and putting them in a net. I asked them why they were filling the balloons and told me it was for some event for the mall.

"Why didn't they call us?" I asked my wife sadly.

It didn't make sense to me. We are the only shop that sells balloons in the mall. Why did they go for an outside shop? After all we did for the mall at the party!

Balloon Order

"This must be our lucky day", my wife said with a big smile on her face
"Why? How much did we sell, yesterday?" I asked.
"We sold no more than usual, but a lady made a balloon decoration order, yesterday", my wife replied.

We were open for over 3 months and until now, we haven't had any outside orders. We were consumed by balloons and toys and forgot about our core business idea, which was to make money making balloon decorations for baby shower parties.

We had been trying to market for that purpose but hadn't succeeded in receiving a response , up until now.

"May be the customer saw the decorations Lia had done, last week", I said referring to the following decoration.

It was simple, but I thought it was very beautiful

The Graduation party

"Great! What did she order?" I asked my wife.
"She selected the picture from the graduation party in our catalogue"

We did make a catalogue showing balloons decorations, but most of the pictures were taken from the Internet. We didn't have our own pics, you see.

The customer selected a nice decoration for graduation party.

"Can Lia do that?" I wondered.
"Well, she better be able to, because she took the order and the advance", my wife said firmly.

The money was good, Lia quoted the customer $300.

Graduation party - 2

The next day my wife came to me and gave me her phone.

"Here, take a look at this", she said angrily.

"What is this?" I asked
"The order Lia made, yesterday"
"But, it looks awful!"
"I know!"
"It's like it was done by me."
"I know!"
"What do you mean, you know?" I asked.

She didn't reply.

"Well?"
"Well, what?"
"What did the customer say?"

"I don't know. I was so upset that I didn't even ask Lia if she got paid"
"Do you think she will pay for this?" I said.
"Well, we did make what she asked for and used many balloons."
"She has to pay", she added adamantly.

After a while, my wife's phone rang.

"This is the third time I received a call from this strange numbe, wait a second." she answered.

"So who was it?" I asked, slightly amused.
"Ha-ha! Very funny! You know who it was." She replied

My wife was very upset. I guess she said the word "sorry" over 20 times during her call with the customer. Was it Lia's mistake or ours that we took a job that we could not handle? Either way, after that incident we got no more decoration orders, which was fine by my wife and I.

The piggy tail

"I told you she doesn't respect me", my wife said in frustration.
"Who doesn't? Oh, do you mean Lia?" I said with a surprise on my face
"Of course, who else could I be talking about?"
"What happened?"
"The piggy tails, she doesn't do them even though I told her many times"

"Dear, it's not a big deal. She has many other things to focus on"

"Like making the balloons in the garage. It's so hot there, I am actually thinking of installing a fan there."

A fan! Why don't you install an air condition for the poor lady? And while you at it, install a TV and bring a sofa.

"Ouch!!"

"And how many times did I make balloons in the afternoon? Did you offer to install a fan for me? No. And all the balloons I made had a piggy tail" She added.

Ouch!!, Again

"You always tell me to focus on details. do you remember the story you told me about McDonald's?" She said, still angry

She was right. A piggy tail is a small thing but I always told her that small things are what make the difference. I told her about the founder of McDonald's driving around his restaurant and picking any of his restaurant bags that were littered. Just to preserve the restaurant image.

"So are you going to talk to her or not?" she asked.

The piggy tails did appear for the next week or so. Then they disappeared.

Section 5

What Am I doing?

·····•◆•·····

Father and Son

I was busy looking for new toys and ideas for the kiosk.

"If you don't give him enough attention, He will look for it elsewhere." she said.

Her statement captured my attention. She was right; I need to spend more time with the kids. Let me start by making it up to my son.

The Rotating Top -1

I took him to the largest toy shop in the city

After less than a minute he came back to me.

I knew that this store was expensive, but $20 for a small toy that just spins on the floor? That was too much, but I wasn't going to break his heart.

The Rotating Top -2

My wife told me our son had been talking about this toy non-stop for the past 2 weeks.

"When I take him to school, I hear all the kids talking about it, there is a TV show about it, or something." she said.

The Rotating Top -3

The very next day I was in the wholesale market to buy more stock, and guess what:

I found it in one shop.

I knew it. I paid too much for that toy. I opened one piece and the quality was indistinguishable from the one I bought for $20.

I bought half a dozen, not to sell it in the kiosk, but for my son to play with and as a proof to my wife of how big the profits businessmen are taking in.

The Rotating Top - 4

The week after that, I made another visit to the wholesale market.

When I checked my mobile phone, I found 5 missed calls from Lia.

I called my wife.

"Did you give the rotating tops to Lia?" I asked.
"Yes, I kept one for our son and gave her the rest to sell", she answered.

"Well, she just told me that she needs more." I said.
"She sold all the ones she had yesterday for $15 apiece", my wife said.

15$ apiece? That's a 12 dollar profit. I immediately bought two dozen.

The Rotating Top -5

A few days later, Lia called me.

"Sir, when are you going to the market? I need more tops."

The next time I went to the market I bought 6 dozen, just to make her stop calling me every few days.

A week later, she called again

"Sir, when are you going to the market? I need more tops."

I ended up buying a full carton which had 48 dozen inside. That's 576 pieces. The box was so big, I had to have it delivered to my house for $50.

Lia was very excited about the rotating tops. They were hot selling and reminded me to buy more and more every time I visited the wholesale market.

"The rotating top is selling like crazy and we are making very good money", I said to my wife.
"All because of our son", my wife replied.

"If they were counterfeits, they would not be selling them in the wholesale market", My wife replied confidently

"Besides, they are only toys, who counterfeits toys?" she added.

I was happy with her answer. I didn't give it another thought. We were making very good money.

Schools are opening

The excitement from the balloon shop experience made me forget about my situation. To put this simply: I was unemployed! However, I had managed to push this fact to the back of my mind. I had good savings and the kiosk occupied all of my time.

The shop made enough money to pay for utilities, groceries and entertainment.

But that didn't last for long. Schools were only a few weeks from opening.

Wow, $8000, I didn't expect to be able to pay tuitions from the shop; nevertheless, the amount reminded me that without a salary I would have to dig deep into my savings.

Unfortunately, the biggest blow came one Monday morning in the form of an SMS:

That was the second payment for the stand rent.

The Vanilla and Schoolbags

"School is opening soon, we didn't buy bags for our kids", my wife told me one morning.

I volunteered to take them because I wanted to buy something from the mall.

Needless to say, after seeing the prices I didn't buy the schoolbags.

"Oh, they were very expensive, I will take them to another shop where prices are cheaper", I told my wife as if I didn't do anything wrong.

But then my eyes brightened up and my voice was filled with excitement.

"But you know what, I bought a Vanilla-scented perfume, you know why?"

I didn't wait for her to answer.

"See, I read in one marketing book, that the smell of vanilla actually encourages people to buy more because it gives them a sense of relaxation", I said.

She didn't answer; she just kept staring at me.

I gave the perfume to Lia and told her to spray it near the kiosk.

"What are you doing?" my wife asked.
"Just what do you think you are doing?", she asked again, raising her voice louder this time.
"What do you mean, this idea will..." she didn't wait for me to complete my sentence.
"I am taking the kids to buy them schoolbags", she said while leaving.

What am I doing?

My life was exciting; I opened a business, which got me a new life. I got to meet new people, understand how money is made out of small businesses and I traveled to china for business. Also, not having a job made me have all the time I need for myself. I was happy, or was I?

284

The excitement of the balloon shop started to wear down, even going to the mall and wholesale market started to become dull.

When school opened I really got bored, not to mention, very lonely.

What was really bothering me though, was money. After paying for my kid's school tuition, I started to realize that the balloon shop would never support me and my family. I was sustaining my standard of living through eating up my savings.

I started to focus more and more on money. I started to do things I didn't do before

I even started to sell things in the kiosk that I would not buy for my kids like "tomatoes":

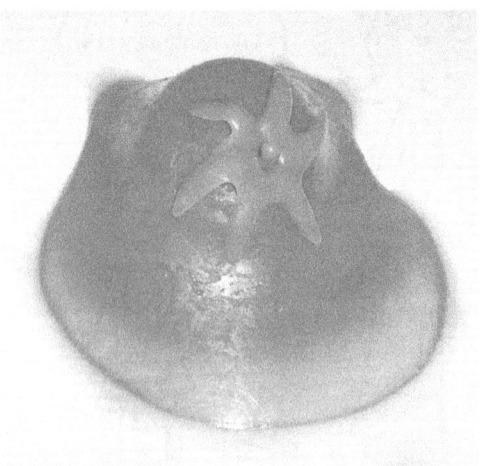

They were squishy, slimy and disgusting, but they were selling very well.

That was something that I perceived to be below my ethics and standards

I was starting to get affected, psychologically. Strange thoughts started to came to me. What if I get into a simple car accident? How will I be labeled?

THE Daily NEWS

TOP STORY

An unemployed man gets into a car accident.

I will be the "unemployed man". My head was hurting every time I thought about being without a job. It was hurting to the degree that I was daydreaming of putting ice on my head.

Was I playing with my kid's future?
I needed to find a job.

Section 6
Back to Work

........••••........

A new job

Do you remember that job advertisement my wife told me about?

I did look at that ad when my wife left. Even though I was busy with the shop at that time and all the money it was making, but still in the back of my mind I knew I couldn't support my family out of its profits, alone. I didn't tell my wife I applied for it. My ego prevented me. The job paid less than the one I quit, but now, having no salary for nearly 6 months, it was time to silence my ego for a moment.

The new job came at just the right time. I had many bills to pay, and even though salary was less than before, it was still quite good.

Pizza

I went back to work and was again quickly dragged back into office life. Wake up early morning, search for a place to have a quick lunch and carry work home.

I was the new employee and wanted to prove myself. Kids were busy at school, which justified for me spending extra hours at work.

Perhaps 3 weeks had passed before I realized that I hadn't had a family dinner since starting the new job.

We decided to order Pizza.

I didn't have cash on me so I went searching in the dresser drawers.

There were many unopened envelops from the kiosk sale.

"Strange! Why didn't my wife open them?" I wondered.

That was strange because we used to open each and every sales' envelope and talk about the sales and then arrange the money in a leather bag I bought from Thailand. In any case I opened one envelope.

There was money in other envelops and I paid for the pizza, but this family dinner was going to be anything but a relaxing one. I had to do a serious talk with my wife.

Serious Talk

My wife was surprise at my question.

"Ah, I don't know, but the envelopes are in the dresser drawer", she answered.
"The envelopes are in the dresser's drawer! Of course they are in the dresser's drawer", I said impatiently.
 "And why have they not been opened, if I might ask?"
"What do you mean?"
"I mean, just because I am back to work and have a salary, that doesn't mean we should neglect the kiosk. I put too much effort in it", I said.
"You !? What about me? I put more effort than you, so stop accusing me of neglecting the kiosk", she replied.

Now it was the time for the kids to leave, a pizza war was about to start.

"Don't change the subject. There was only $5 in one

envelope. Why didn't you check the sales?"

It took her 1 millisecond to respond back.

"No, you don't change the subject. When was the last time you went to check on the kiosk?" she shot back.

Three weeks. Yes, I hadn't been to the kiosk, since I started my new job. It was because I was busy, but perhaps the main reason was that I had grown bored of the kiosk. The novelty of the experience had worn off.

"You know I am busy with the new job", I said, defending myself.
"I am also busy with the kids' school", she responded.
"Do you think that is easy? Watching your son at the soccer match searching for his father is not easy", she added ferociously.

She wasn't backing down and neither was I. After one hour we came to an agreement:

We put too much effort into the kiosk,
We must not waste all our hard work

Checking on Lia

The next day we went to check on Lia.

I was very upset. Furious, actually. How come the shop is empty, especially now that I can afford to buy more stock than ever before? I think this was the first time I raise my voice at Lia.

Now my wife entered the shouting match

"You are lying! You didn't tell me anything."
"Yes I did, madam. I sent you an SMS!"

"She didn't call me, maybe she sent a message, but my phone is filled with messages, I cannot check every single one I get!" my wife said.

Everybody in the mall was looking at us.

To be honest, I wasn't upset about the money we lost from losing potential sales.

I was upset because these were mistakes that beginners would make, and I thought that we were beyond that stage.

There was no use trying to figure out who was at fault between Lia, my wife and me.

That same day, I went to the wholesale market and spent 3,000 dollars on toys.

I bought so many toys that I had to drive all the way back with some toys on my lap. If the police had seen me, I am sure I would have spent the night at jail.

Take more care Lia

Even though I had an early meeting tomorrow, I spent the night with my wife and Lia arranging all the stuff I bought. The kiosk came back to life

Before I leave, I wanted to express my disappointment
with Lia but in a soft way.

My wife started to laugh.

My face turned red and yelled to her "Do you find this funny?"

When Lia walked away, she said.

Police

I went to work full of energy the next day. I was getting some excitement back from the shop. Now that I have a paying job, I can buy more stock for the kiosk. I can even take another trip to China. I started to daydream at my desk of buying a container from china filled with toys and balloons, until my mobile started ringing.

"A customer wanted to order balloons, I don't have time to do this", I thought.

Before I told the guy that we don't take balloons orders, he hit me with:

My heart fell into my stomach. The police? Why would they be asking me about the shop? What did Lia do? Did she get into a fight with some customers? Even so, what do I have to do with this? She is responsible for her own actions.

"Your shop is under investigation, you need to come in for questioning." He told me on the phone.
"W .. Wh .. Why? What's wrong?" I asked in a shaky voice.
"You will know when you come to the station", the caller replied with authority.

What happened?

Do you think Lia did something?" my wife asked.

"I don't know, They refused to give me any details on the phone."

I called Lia.

If it wasn't Lia, then who or what was it?

"If it was something serious, they wouldn't have just called you. They would have sent a police care to pick you up." my wife said trying to comfort me.
"Arrest me? The shop is under your name, you are responsible", I replied angrily.
"So, now I am responsible? I had nothing to do with the shop since you took sides with Lia", she said.
"No! If I go down, you go down with me", I replied.

We were talking like drug dealers waiting to be arrested, but neither of us had been involved with the police, before.

That night there was no TV, no dinner and no sleep. There were only bad thoughts and nightmares.

Police station

It was my first time at any police station.

My heart was pounding and had difficulty breathing. I took a seat and was called to a windowless office.

"How long will I stay? Are they going to make me stay for the night?" I asked the detective sitting behind the desk. "There is a company that filed a complaint that your establishment is selling fake goods with their trademark", the detective said.
"Estab... Establishment? We don't even have a shop, we only have a small kiosk in the mall", I replied.

The detective threw some photos at me of the rotating tops we had been selling in the kiosk.

It was the money-making rotating tops we bought so cheaply from the wholesale market. I knew it was going to get us into trouble.

"I am sorry, it was a mistake, we didn't mean to, I told my wife we shouldn't buy them.." I kept on giving excuses and my eyes started to get watery.

"Judge? That means there will be court". I was so scared that I was barely able to walk out of the detective's office.

What we are going to do?

"He told me, the court date is in a week", I told my wife.
"Did he tell you to get a lawyer", my wife asked.
"He said that it's up to me."
"You know lawyers are very expensive", she said.
"Yes, I know…"

After a few minutes of silence, she said, "Why don't you just tell the judge that Lia bought the toys and that she is the one that needs to be punished?" my wife said.

I didn't respond. Lia did tell me to buy the tops more than once, but I could have refused. To be honest I kept thinking about that point.

I stared to search the law on selling fake goods.

The receipts - 1

"If we can show the court that we bought the tops from the wholesale market, they might let us off the hook", I said.

"That's a great idea", my wife said excited.
"OK, quickly, bring me all the bills we have for the tops", I told my wife.
"But you didn't give me any receipts lately", she said with the excitement slipping off her face.

She was correct. My trips to the wholesale market became so frequent, that I stopped caring about receipts.

I felt that I had developed good intuition about selling toys to know which ones will sell and for how much. When my wife would ask me for receipts, I would just tell her that we didn't need them.

"We are beyond the need for receipts. We can price toys from our experience and use our intuition!" I used to tell her.

I also thought that I had become well-known in the wholesale market and was building a trusting relationship with the salespeople.

"But we bought so many tops, there must be some receipts", my wife said.

If there were some receipts left, they would be in the old box I used to throw every paper related to the shop in.

The receipts - 2

"Why don't you go and buy more tops?" my wife suggested.

"Just be nice and ask for receipts. Act as if nothing had happened", she advised me.

The next day, I immediately headed to the wholesale market after work.

The salesman, who I knew very good acted as if he didn't know what I was talking about.

I took my wife's advice and stayed calm

"I bought a few dozen about three weeks ago, can you check your records? I need a copy of the receipt for accounting purposes", I said in the most pleasant voice "Sorry sir, I don't remember you." The man said in a loud voice and quickly retreated to the back of the shop.

The court day

I didn't hire a lawyer. I reasoned that if the judge sees me with a lawyer he would think that I am one of those rich businessmen who think that they are above the law.

I had a strategy:
- I will address him as, 'your honor'.

- I will explain to him, that we bought the toys in broad dayight from the wholesale market.

If all else fails, I will cry and beg.

The ruling

"So what happened? You came home early." my wife asked when I came back from the court.

"The judge said, he was lenient because this was our first offence", I told my wife.

"And the last one", she said quickly.

"And the last one", I repeated after her.

To be honest, I was happy about the ruling. $1500 is a lot more than what we made from selling the fake tops, but at least we didn't have to pay quarter of a million dollars.

Lia and Customers - Just Let it Go

After the court ordeal finished, I felt emotionally drained. For now, I just wanted to focus on my new job, save some money and then think about another visit to China.

I was seated at my desk checking my emails when the phone started ringing.

Lia was calling, but I didn't have time for her. My inbox was full of emails, so I didn't answer.

But she kept calling and calling, so I finally picked p.

I knew this was big, Lia's voice was shaking which was totally out of character for her.

"Her boy took a light ball and didn't pay for it", she told me.

I told Lia to tell the security. I already had a discussion with her about not getting involved in any conflict with customers and leave that to the security.

"Sir, she told the security she brought the ball from home."

I wanted to hang up, but she kept talking.

"Sir, I am sure that her kid took it from the stand", she added.
"Ok, Lia, listen to me, its not a problem. Let it go, it cost me less than 50 cents to buy", I said, trying to calm her down.

But Lia didn't let it go, of course.

"Sir, her husband has came and shouted at me."

I took a moment to add things up, I know that if someone has shouted at Lia, she will not let it pass

"And what did you do?" I asked.
"I shouted back and took the ball. Sir, I am not lying", she said.

But this wasn't about truth anymore, it's becoming more serious.

"OK, what happened next?"
"The man said he was going to complain about me"

Immediately I calculated the situation; if the customer complained about Lia, the mall management will tell me to let her go.

I told Lia to immediately take a full box of balls and give

it to the customer as a gift, just don't let him complain. I told her to run before he reaches the management office.

Goodbye Lia

For one hour I was constantly watching my phone. I prayed that the mall will not call me, but they did. I had a lengthy talk with *Mr. G* and before he hanged up, he told me:

"Three days? How can we find a worker in only 3 days", my wife wondered.

I'm sorry Lia, I can't help you. You must find another job.

I felt very sad for Lia. We were together for almost a year and she never missed a day of work. Even when she was sick, she would only take a couple of hours to go to the doctor then return to the stand. As for my wife, I couldn't believe it but I actually saw a few tears in her eyes.

A replacement for Lia

Finding a replacement wasn't very difficult this time. We weren't looking for a balloons artist, rather a salesperson. In addition, the kiosk was already setup.

One Year passed

When Lia left us, almost a year had passed. Now was the time to calculate how much profit we made. I left that task to my wife.

I was happy, very happy.

"Not to mention, we even had the fun experience of being sued for selling counterfeit toys.", she added sarcastically

My wife stood up and asked the question I knew she wanted to ask long time ago.

"Do I want to continue?"
"Of course, even if we made only one dollar, it would be enough for me", I said without hesitation.

I was very excited and started to tell my wife about my plans for growing the business.

"Wow, you are definitely very excited, even after all the trouble we went through", she said.

"But tell me one thing, so now do you know the secret of small businesses?"

"Yes", I answered.

Section 7

Few Things
We Learned

················•◆•◆•◆•················

Everyone's dream

You are not the only one. It's everyone dream to own his/her own business and have financial freedom. But I think you know that, so what's my point? My point is: the competition is very hard. You are basically competing with everyone from housewives to football players to CEOs

It's not all yours

When Lia brought the money I thought it was all "profit" and was spending it like it was all mine.

But that money was only "sales" not profit. Profit is only a part of sale because you will have to use part (a big part) of sales money to buy new stock, pay salaries and rent.

You need to sell high

When I bought a toy for 1 dollar and sold it for 7, I thought I was cheating people. But I wasn't thinking that I was paying 25,000 for a wooden stand plus other expenses.

If you discovered that a business is selling products much higher than they bought it for think of their costs.

I am not saying that some business doesn't put way too much markup on their prices, but just to put things into perspective.

Don't always lower your prices

Lowering your prices is one strategy to beat the competition (of course). However, it will cause you to earn less profit. Try to get the max profit you can and look for other ways to beat the competition like a better service.

Keep your secrets

They say: A magician never tells his secret. It is the same for businesses. They will not tell you their secrets like from where they buy their stock and how much profit they make. I was wondering why and didn't understand until I experienced running the balloon shop.

A lot of research and effort goes into finding products and pricing. Many mistakes will be made along the way (which cost money), so why should they tell their secrets? It's actually part of the game to discover secrets.

It is about money

Please save yourself and everyone around you the trouble and don't say your goal from your business is not money. If you don't want money or you think it's evil (which is absolutely not) then that's your opinion and you are entitled to it. But your business will need money, period. Even if your business is a charity you will need the cash to pay the workers and grow the business.

Discuss your idea

It might be amazing in your mind, but you will never know until you discuss it.

Write your idea

Even after you discuss your idea with someone you trust, write it down. Writing a business case is not a waste of time. I thought that until I sat down with my wife to write the business plan for the balloon shop. Having to write what we wanted to do made us realize how little we understood our idea.

Get a partner

I was fortunate to have my wife as a partner. Select someone you trust and have traits that compensate for your gaps. My wife was better in managing money and focusing on details, which helped the balloon shop a lot.

It's a difficult journey; find someone to share the good and the bad with.

There will be conflicts

When we first started the balloon shop there were fewer conflicts between me and my wife. I had two failed attempts before and was open to ideas and suggestion. But with time I was less open minded to my wife suggestions and conflicts increased especially on how to manage Lia.

To be honest, the only reason for me was "ego". With time, I thought I became an expert in running a business and viewed any suggestion from my wife that contradict what I think is correct as a personal attack.

So how can you manage this? The answer is simple: by managing your ego, but that's certainly not simple. In any case and at the end, running a small business is not much mathematics as it is opinions and ideas.

Don't make it personal

At the end of the story, you saw how the kiosk had very less stock. That was at the time when I was employed again and was able to afford to buy more stock than ever.

The reason was my wife wasn't communicating with Lia. The friction between them made us lose money from the potential sale.

Roles and responsibilities

Going back to the earlier point of not having enough stock:

Why didn't Lia contact me if she needed more stock?

Why didn't my wife visit the kiosk?

Why didn't I visit the kiosk?

We all assumed that the other person will do it. If we had clear rules and responsibilities this might never happen.

Who cares the most about your business?

Going back to the earlier point you would expect that Lia should keep calling me day and night to ask for more stock. After all, she is the one who is directly involved in the kiosk. The answer came clear (and true) from my wife even though she was laughing at me. She said, " No one will care about your business more than you"

327

Opening a business is still work

How naive I was to think that running a small business is easier than being employed. On the contrary, being employed is 10 times easier.

You will need to make the decisions

Working as an employee you most likely had policies, procedures, and supervisors telling you what to do. However, in running a business no one will tell you what to do. It will be all your responsibility from major things like choosing a location to lease your shop to simple things like deciding on the color of your logo. And these decisions you make will either help you make or lose money (your money).

It's so complex

Running a business is a complex task. By complex, I mean that there are so many different factors you need to consider in taking decisions.

For example, before buying a toy you can consider its price, quality, novelty and fun factor. But even after doing all the research, you can't be 100% sure it will sell good because it is nearly impossible to identify all the factors. For example, what about the income level of people living in the area? season? perceived value? culture? etc.

Develop your "Gut Feeling"

This is linked to the earlier point.

So what to do about it? How can you select the product that will sell? Well, in the balloon shop, I found that for the toys I buy after having a "gut" feeling that they will sell good were in fact selling better that the toys I try to concisely think about their selling potential. Of course, this wasn't always the case but in most cases.

This is not to discount planning and research, on the contrary, they will build your gut feeling.

The conclusion I came to is to try to do as much research and planning in your business to reach a point where your subconscious makes the decisions for you. Does it make sense to you? I hope so.

Your business will not save you from "office politics"

I quit my day job because someone else got the promotion that I felt I am entitled to. I was upset of course and said: "Life is unfair".

I thought that having my own business (i.e. working for my self) will solve this problem. I know many people share the same hope because that was the only way out when I discussed office politics with my colleagues at work.

Unfortunately, I am sad to report that unless you open your business in a cave you will still have to deal with government agencies, competitors, and vendors. And more than likely you will face situations where you will feel you were treated unfairly.

Market research

"Market Research" is a big word that used to intimidate me, but I found out that it can be easily done. Just drive around and visit stores that sell similar stuff to what you plan to.

My wife made me visit as many baby shower stores before we started and I believe it made a big difference; because I developed a feeling for prices and what customers want.

Competition is not always bad

When my wife told me that there were other shops selling baby shower items my immediate thought was to find another idea. But she insisted on continuing with the idea and didn't think much of the competition.

Don't be afraid of competition, having other shops in the same business is an indicator that there is a market for it. Of course, competition can be so strong that there is little money to be made, but what I am trying to say is that a little competition is not bad and might actually help you to succeed.

Start selling ASAP

We started selling from the first day we opened. This brought excitement and a much-needed confidence into the business.

Imagine if we didn't sell at the beginning? How disappointed we would be? Especially after all the effort we had put in.

But we weren't selling anything special and the main reason we were selling was because we rented a place in a mall with good foot traffic.

Foot traffic is vital

Many of us hate crowded places. But for business, this is exactly what you should be looking for.

The more people pass by your shop the more chance of selling you will have. Don't rent a place in an area that doesn't get enough people going there because the rent is cheap. Remember rent prices differ for a reason.

You will need to get licensed

There are 3 implications to having to get licensed

1- It will cost you money (maybe thousands) so you need to consider it in your total investment

2- It can be time-consuming.

3- You might have a restriction on your business idea. Expect anything to happen from denying you to use the business name you want to not even approving your business idea.

It really depends on the country you live in and the type of business you selected

Public safety

When we first started we didn't tie balloons when we sold them. This, of course, made it easy for the balloons to escape from the small hands of our customers

Our solution was to tie them of course. We decided to use small candles because they looked good and were cheap (10 cents a piece).

However, one evening we got a call from an angry customer saying her young daughter was eating the wax off the candle. She threatened to call the public safety.

Thankfully she didn't call but we had to change our approach. We started using plastic rings but they were relatively expensive at 30 cents a piece.

Know the law

Running a business WILL expose you to new laws that you need to comply with. One of them is copyrights law. You saw in the story how selling a counterfeit product can get you in serious legal problems.

You need to understand that a business is treated more strictly by law enforcement agencies. For example, buying a counterfeit product for your personal use is treated less harshly that selling the same counterfeit product

Temptation and ethics

It's easy to label people as greedy and unethical when you don't experience the pressure of temptation they face. We faced many temptations to make easy money by selling products we will not allow our kids to buy. One of them was selling laser pointers, which was selling like hot cakes and we could make up to 500% profit. We were happy that we didn't continue to sell them, but it wasn't easy.

Buying is psychological

I loved shopping and was spending lots of money buying things I needed and many things I didn't need. However, after starting the balloon shop my urge of buying was significantly reduced. I felt satisfied buying stuff from the wholesale market even though I was selling them and not for my personal use.

So, for me, it was buying for the sake of buying not for the actual need of the product. That was a positive thing I learned from the balloon shop.

334

Are customers always right ?

I have been a customer the whole of my life. I complained about cold soup, bad service, and uncooperative staff. However, when the time came to be on the other side I discovered how some people can be a real pain. After having to let Lia go because a customer complaint about her I became more considerate and tolerating toward salespeople. They work long shifts and have to deal with different people. Their salary is also not that great. They are human being and can have bad days. So be little compassionate to that

You might have more than one supplier

In many small businesses, you will need suppliers. Chances are you will have the same (or similar) product that you need from different suppliers with different pricing. So don't rush, take your time researching.

Researching is not easy

This is linked to the earlier point. Researching for a product is not easy. Imagine you are looking for a teddy bear in one of the wholesale markets in China. There are literally hundreds of shops selling teddy bears with different sizes, quality, and prices. It can take you days to just research on teddy bears (I am not exaggerating). It's different than going shopping for a teddy bear for a birthday party.

Buying wholesale

Buying wholesale is one of running small business fundamentals. When you open a business and need to buy products, always buy them at a discount. Try to get very big discounts. It varies of course from product to product, for some, you can hope for only 10% discount (like smart phones) to up to 90% and more discount for others (like some toys)

But buying wholesale has its disadvantages. You will need to buy a quantity of the same product with some restrictions. For example, if you want to buy a teddy bear from the wholesale market the seller will make you buy a minimum of 10 pieces and if there are 3 different colors you will not be able to choose the one you like (i.e. need to take from all the colors even if you believe one of them will not sell well).

Retail is much nicer than wholesale

The wholesale markets are (usually) missing the nice ambient and arrangements you see in shopping malls. Wholesale markets is not a shopping center, it is a place of work. Just be prepared.

Dealing with employee

It's not easy to manage your employees. After all, they are human beings and will have good day and bad days. Can you keep a professional relationship with them without being too attached and at the same time not to become inhumane?

Many problems can arise if you become too close to your employees because times will come when you will need to discipline them or even fire them. On the other hand, you should always keep a good relationship with them because they are the people who run your business.

Create your HR policies slowly

You will need to set many rules for your workers like when to have a lunch break? What to wear and what not to wear? How to treat customers? What to do if they get sick? ... Etc.

It's better, of course, to write all these things up, but start slowly and add items as they arise because you cannot capture all possible events. For example, my wife and I never thought of what to do with Lia if she overinflates balloons and causes them to explode. Should we deduct money from her salary or just let it go?

Making rules clear

Linked to the earlier point. Do you remember when we found a pickle jar in the kiosk? From our point of view, it is very clear that food is not allowed to be stored in the kiosk. However, from Lia's point of view, it was only a small pickle's jar tucked away from they eyes of the customers.

This is an example of how there are many details that you might miss and you will need to capture them as your business grows.

People will assume you are making profit

People will have the assumption that since you have a business you are making money and will try to take advantage of that. For example, they might approach you to sponsor their events, which is absolutely fine. But be careful of other people who might want to make money out of you like suing you for a product that harmed them in some way or another. Be careful of what you are selling and make sure it is approved by relevant legislations.

Read your leasing agreement carefully

Are you required to pay a deposit? Is it refundable? And most importantly will the rent increase in coming years? You will spend money on decorating and preparing your shop, try to get an agreement in which the rent amount will not increase for few years.

Others will want to sell to you

If you sell something from your shop, do you care if the customer uses it or not? Maybe, but most likely your biggest interest will be in just selling. Likewise, other business will want to sell to you and will be indifferent if you are able to sell back what you bought from them. Be careful in the wholesale market if salespeople try to sell you stuff more than what you need. Nobody can guarantee if a product sells or not. Everyone will be looking for his/her business wellbeing.

Playing with the big boys

When we first went to the wholesale market we bought a box of wrapping papers. We only wanted 12 pieces but ended up buying 144 pieces.

We bought a box because we were challenged by the salesperson that we were not a "real" business and are not able to buy big quantity.

Most of the wrapping papers didn't sell.

You will need money to start

This might be a simple observation, but I didn't realize that until the opening day. I spent thousands of dollars on rent, licensing and preparing the kiosk. I also spent thousands buying balloons and toys but still the kiosk didn't look full. I realized then that I needed much more investment than I planned for (and it was only for a small kiosk)

So, be prepared to have funds. Do you want to borrow and get into debt? Maybe?

The excitement will fade away

It will happen one day. I was going daily to the balloon shop and weekly to the wholesale market. But with time I started to spend less and less time at the shop to the point that weeks passed by before I visited.

So be prepared by enabling your business to run with the minimum intervention from you as soon as possible. One way to do that is by hiring a dedicated manager and having progress reports.

Buying more or less

In the wholesale market, the more you buy the better deal you get. For example, a dozen of teddy bear can cost you 50 $ but a carton of 6 dozens can cost you only 45 $ a dozen.

My advice is to always test the product and buy the minimum quantity you are allowed to and not to be tempted by the further discount. But it's not that simple, what if it is a new product and you have one chance to order? Well, sometimes you need to take risks.

"Copy, Paste" management concepts

Be careful when you read about business studies in management books. Many of these studies were done in big companies that have funds and experience that your business might not have.

Don't jump into applying these studies to your business until you determine that your business is in a similar maturity and can actually benefit from them.

Get quality information

Our son told us about the rotating top. And it was selling like crazy. Get your information from your customers or those who resemble them. Be careful from the mindset of " I know better of what they want"

People buy more in holidays!

The balloons shop used to sell 4-5 times more during weekends than in normal days. In holidays, the sale can reach up to 10 times more. Be prepared for holidays by stocking more and new products

Relationships

You need to build good relationships with your vendors. With good relationships, you can get easy payment (many businesses who buy from the wholesale market buy with credit). Also, you get early notice of new and limited and you might also get a discount.

Know where your business is at

When I first started buying toys from the wholesale market I focused on small and inexpensive toys like yo-yos and springs. With time, however, I started to bring more quality toys, the ones that are similar in quality to those sold in high-end toy stores. But they were not selling very good even though they were cheaper and of similar quality.

What I wasn't doing right is to understand people perception of the shop and if they trust buying expensive stuff from it. Maybe it wasn't worth it for them to save 5 or 10 dollars and buy from a place that doesn't even have an exchange policy.

Shelf life

The items you sell might expire and cause you to lose money. During the first week of opening the shop we were selling more balloons every day but after the first weekend there were balloons lying all around the kiosk.

This caused a dilemma for me and my wife: we needed to make as many balloons as we can because it will attract customers, on the other hand, if no one bought them we will lose money.

Everything will fall out of fashion

People get tired of seeing the same stuff again and again. To maintain successful selling try to always bring new product and sell them before they fall out of fashion

Mastering business

It will never happen. You will be always learning and some days you will make a big profit and some days you will lose money. Keep an open mind; you will definitely become better at it with time.

346

www.ingramcontent.com/pod-product-compliance
Lightning Source LLC
Chambersburg PA
CBHW051624170526
45167CB00001B/51